# The Last Years of British Rail
# 1990-94

# The Last Years of British Rail 1990-94

## John Stretton

· BRITISH RAILWAYS COLLECTION ·

© John Stretton 2003

First published in 2003

British Library Cataloguing in Publication D

A catalogue record for this book is availabl
Library.

ISBN 1 85794 216 7

*Frontispiece* This book is a reflection on the final years of British Rail, and here we have a reflection of No 47063 on shed at Tinsley on 16 September 1993. Increasingly cash-strapped during its latter years, BR was so often forced to 'make do and mend', leading to less than ideal situations, epitomised by the condition of 47063's surroundings.

Originating in Crewe Works in January 1965 as D1647 and initially working from Newport (Ebbw Junction) shed, it was renumbered to 47063 in February 1974 and finally withdrawn from Tinsley some 20 years later on 22 September 1995. M. R. J. Phillips administered the last rites – cutting it up at Crewe Works during February 1997. *MJS*

# Acknowledgements

As with any book, there are many people 'in the background' who play a vital part in the completion of the whole, while the author – as 'front man' – takes the glory. In this particular volume, the undoubted heroes are the far-sighted and gifted photographers who have allowed their work to be showcased herein. The 'gang of four' who thus deserve credit here are – in alphabetical order! – Tom Heavyside, Colin Marsden, Brian Morrison and Ray Ruffell. The remainder of illustrations, with a credit of *MJS*, are mine.

In addition, credit and thanks must go to my wife Judi, who has tolerated long periods of isolation as I either sit huddled gnome-like in front of the computer or peer at innumerable photographs. Without her forbearance I could not have achieved the task within even the third deadline! Finally, to Peter Townsend at Silver Link for putting up with those first two deadlines being missed, to David and Anna in the Silver Link office for their unflinching patience and courtesy, and to Will Adams and Mick Sanders for their usual skilful and speedy editing and design. Thank you all!

# Bibliography

Baker, S. K. *Rail Atlas Great Britain & Ireland*
*British Railways Pre-Grouping Atlas & Gazetteer* (Ian Allan)
Butlin, Ashley *British Multiple Units* Vol 1 DMUs and DEMUs; Vol 2 EPBs, Haps, Saps & Caps; Vol 3 Classes 302-390
McManus, Michael *Locomotive Stock Changes* Vol 6 Diesel & Electric 1948-68
Marsden, Colin *The Complete BR Diesel & Electric Locomotive Directory*

Rhodes, Michael *The Illustrated History of Marshalling Yards*
Wignall, C. J. *British Railways Maps & Gazetteer 1825-1985*

Various issues of *Rail* magazine for 1990-94
Various issues of *Rail Express* magazine for relevant 'Rattle & Roll Years'

# Contents

Just ten days into Privatisation, and the new owners are keen to establish that BR is no more. As can be seen on 10 April 1994, this was now Railtrack's domain, clearly signposted outside King's Cross station. *MJS*

# Introduction

On 8 January 1990 Sir Robert Reid, British Rail's outgoing Chairman, gave a speech to the Chartered Institute of Transport, outlining progress over the previous decade and the change to a business-led industry, and calling for direct investment from the Government, rather than the railway being allowed to spend its own money. Needless to say, in hindsight, he was whistling in the wind, with a Tory Government ruled over during that period by the Iron Lady, who boasted that she never travelled by rail. However, change was still afoot and a lot happened over the final five years to Privatisation on 1 April 1994.

Within these pages I have shone a spotlight on this last period of British Rail, highlighting both new and old, the innovations and the everyday, but with the focus on the aesthetic rather than merely the 'record shot'. No attempt is being made to provide a definitive review of the period, rather a snapshot of events as recorded by some of the country's leading photographers. The layout of the book is chronological, in the same fashion as used in my earlier look at the operations of BR in its latter days, *Closely Observed Trains* (Silver Link Publishing, 1994). Covering the period 1980-89, that volume has been long out of print, but was well enough received to spawn this 'Volume 3', for the earlier book is to be republished in two separate volumes, updated and with additional material. So if you missed it the first time around, you will be in for a treat – and even if you are lucky enough to have a copy, you will not be disappointed with what will effectively become Volumes 1 and 2, released in this new style.

◀ One of the last innovations from BR was the introduction of a new generation of DMUs, now universally known as the 'Turbos'. Displaying a route code and suitable destination display – bearing in mind the area over which these units were to be introduced – class leader No 165001 enjoys the limelight of a laser show during its launch at BREL Works in York on 15 February 1991. The final set of 76 built – 39 165/0s and 37 165/1s – was No 165137, delivered from ABB's York Works on 9 December 1992. *Brian Morrison*

Ironically, bearing in mind the comment in my first paragraph, 1990 saw the demise of Mrs Thatcher as Prime Minister and leader of the Conservative Party, with her resignation in November. The Poll Tax revolts earlier in the year obviously did not help! This was also the year of the breakout of Mad Cow Disease, Saddam Hussein invading Kuwait, and gale force winds causing chaos, but also, on happier notes, Nelson Mandela being released after 27 years in prison, the re-unification of Germany, and British and French tunnellers meeting under the Channel. On the railways, it was the last year of Class 50s out of Paddington – replaced by ex-Scottish 47s – but also the appearance of the first Class 158 unit on test and then in service on the Glasgow-Edinburgh route, the last Class 90 built, and the first Class 60 accepted into traffic. ARC introduced its Class 59/1s, and there were livery changes for the Civil Engineer's department and Parcels sector. A number of locomotives were put into store, but overall the year was a quiet one for both withdrawals and introductions.

1991 opened with 'Desert Storm', the military drive to liberate Kuwait and crush the Iraqi army in January, and the now infamous 'wrong kind of snow', creating major problems, for the operation of passenger services especially, during February. Robert Maxwell was drowned off the Canary Islands and other deaths included Freddie Mercury, John Arlott, Dames Margot Fonteyn and Peggy Ashcroft, Graham Greene and Miles Davis. It was also the end for heavy rail on the Altrincham-Manchester line, Speedlink, loco-hauled trains on the Trans-Pennine route, Barrow Hill depot, the Diesel Repair Shop at Stratford, Classes 81 and 85, and Vic Berry's scrapyard in Leicester, after a disastrous fire. Elsewhere, unit 303048 was repainted in original 'Blue Train' livery, Rail express systems (Res) was born, there was a celebration of the 150th anniversary of the Brighton line, the innovative Charterail service was launched by Petfoods – and then abandoned when costs were too high! – and electric services between King's Cross and Edinburgh started in the summer. On the loco front, the influx of accepted Class 60s saw the withdrawal of many older types, but a relatively young 56042 was also dispensed with, due to its non-standard CP1 bogies.

The 12 months of 1992 were summed up by HM the Queen as an 'annus horribilis', but no doubt John Major did not agree, securing a second term as Prime Minister in April, against all the odds and pundits. Both Paddy Ashdown and David Mellor were in the news for 'affairs', Mike Tyson was jailed for rape, the Coal Board announced proposals to close 31 pits, and Frankie Howerd and Benny Hill died. Ravenscraig steelworks and Bilston Glen and Bickershaw collieries closed (among others), together with a fatal accident at Morpeth and the announcement of 5,000 BR jobs to go, all adding to the gloom. The unique Brush Class 89 was withdrawn and Class 50s ceased regular turns on the Waterloo-Exeter route, but elsewhere new liveries were given to four Class 90s and two 26s (as D5300/1), and 165xxx 'Turbos' took over on the Oxford/Newbury routes to Paddington.

1993 was the year that Privatisation was finally announced, following rumours, speculation, dread and widespread fear and loathing at the prospect. One wonders if there was a connection between this and the death of Daisy Adams, Britain's oldest person, at 113! The link to Manchester Airport was completed, as was the Brush Class 60 contract, that firm then moving on to the construction of the 92s, the first of which appeared in this year. Also, the first Eurostar unit ran through the Channel Tunnel, as did the first SNCF loco to work in Britain, at the head of the inaugural passenger working under the water. The first stage of the new 'Robin Hood Line' opened to Newstead in May. New stock was literally 'dropped into' 'The Drain' – the Waterloo & City Line – and new 'Turbo' depots at Salisbury and Reading opened, but on the down side loco-hauled trains ended between Waterloo

and Exeter. It was also the end for the Class 26s, and the deaths were announced of Robert Adley MP, ex-BR Chairman Sir Robert Reid, and Pat Whitehouse (of *Railway Roundabout* fame).

And so to the end – the year of Privatisation and (ironically and appropriately?) the launch of the National Lottery! Tony Blair became the youngest ever leader of the Labour Party and Nelson Mandela South Africa's first black President, while Fred and Rosemary West were charged with murder and O. J. Simpson was on a charge of murdering his wife. Three new companies were forged from BR's Trainload Freight sector and the first of National Power's Class 59/2s arrived in this country. Railtrack was formed on 1 April (perhaps an ominous date considering subsequent events!), the Channel Tunnel finally opened on 6 May, and the first phase of the 'Ivanhoe Line' opened. The Class 323 EMUs finally entered service and D172 *Ixion* became the first preserved diesel to return to the main line. More sadly, Dai Woodham (of Barry Docks fame) and veteran railway author O. S. Nock both died this year, five died in the Cowden crash, and Dover West Docks station and Ripple Lane depot closed.

While BR only lived for three months of 1994, the rest of the year is included in this book, as such a huge undertaking could not possibly disappear overnight. Existing practices and rolling-stock would continue for some time, as can be seen from the images herein contained.

In *Closely Observed Trains* I opined that the decade of 1980-89 had probably seen more change on our railways than any previous similar period. This pace of change did not let up in the five years covered here. These pages have only encapsulated a microcosm of development, but I hope the reader will remember or learn about some of the things that happened and forgive me if I have omitted their pet story or location. But above all, I trust he or she will enjoy the illustrations so brilliantly captured by the various photographers.

# 1990

**4 March**

Perhaps not what might have been expected as the opener for the last five years of British Rail, but one feature of those last years and the immediately preceding period was the increase in steam tours over the main line. In any event, the picture is a superb image in its own right! With full permission, the photographer is standing on a specially provided match wagon to record the unveiling of a plaque commemorating 100 years of the Forth Bridge and to capture this impressive portrait of No 60009 (here running as *Osprey* rather than its true persona of *Union of South Africa*) heading over the southern approach viaduct of the bridge, at the head of 'The Forth Centennial', an Edinburgh-Perth Forth Bridge Centenary special. Emerging from Doncaster Works in June 1937 and withdrawn 29 years later, the loco has carried the glory of Gresley's design to many parts of the network since restoration. *Brian Morrison*

### ▲ 31 March

Coming right up to date, BR's 'brave new world' echoes the front end of the 'A4' seen on the previous page, streamlining again to the fore on the ECML. Just two months old and named *Terence Cuneo* 25 days prior to this view, No 91011 brings up the rear of the 1210 service to King's Cross as it departs from Leeds City, its number being faithfully recorded in the spotter's notebook. Like so many things with our modern railway, however, the name was only transitory, being removed in 1997, but since modification to No 91111 on 12 December 2002, the name has been restored. *Tom Heavyside*

### ▼ 7 April

During the 1980s, BR introduced what came to be known as the 'second generation' DMUs, updating and replacing units that, in many cases, had been around since the immediate aftermath of the Modernisation Plan of 1955. The Class 150 'Sprinters', especially, became ubiquitous throughout the network, performing their day-to-day duties largely unsung and unloved. On this day, No 150107, branded in Provincial Sector livery of light and dark blue, runs under the wires into Stoke station with the 1447 Crewe-Derby service. Note that, unlike so many other locations that were altered almost beyond recognition over the years, not least with the introduction of overhead wires, Stoke has retained its glorious all-over trainshed, with substantial supporting pillars. In the background, two Class 20s stand stabled by the signal box in company with a 31. *Tom Heavyside*

### ▲ 9 April

In contrast to Stoke, the old Dumbarton & Balloch Railway station at Balloch, by the shores of Loch Lomond, received modernisation attention during the late 1980s and is seen here, freshly landscaped and with new station buildings and platform surface. Shoppers laden with full bags detrain from the 1346 service from Airdrie to make their way home, perhaps by way of the parked cars to the left, while the train, formed of units 311108 and 303029, will 'turn round' to form the 1508 to Drumgelloch. At the foot of the steps, a Strathclyde Transport notice warns of attempting to buy tickets on the train when there are facilities at the station! The last Class 311 was rendered extinct in November 1990. *Tom Heavyside*

### ▼ 16 April

One week later, and the focus has moved from north-west of Glasgow to south-west of Perth, to the ex-Caledonian station at Gleneagles, home to the golf course of the same name – another famous landmark on Scotland's tourist trail. While Balloch is at the end of a short branch, Gleneagles is home to the main line between Perth and Glasgow, and the differing style of motive power thus encountered is evidenced here in the shape of No 47604 as it pauses with the 1510 Aberdeen-Glasgow express. Built at Crewe in November 1965, D1972 became 47271 in September 1974, before a further transformation to 47604 in December 1983, to 47674 in July 1991, and, yet again, to 47854 on 24 October 1995. It received *Women's Royal Voluntary Service* nameplates in August 1988 and lost them in May 2003. *Tom Heavyside*

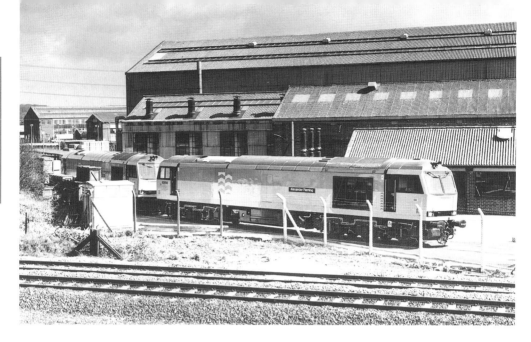

**▲ 16 April**

On the same day that saw Tom Heavyside exploring Scotland and photographing the 'Brush 4', the latest generation of Brush locomotives was making ready to escape the confines of the Loughborough-based factory. In the final 20 years of British Rail, several new classes of (mostly freight) engines were introduced, some being built by outside contractors. The Class 60 from Brush was an innovation over what had gone before and, perhaps not surprisingly, the locos were not without their teething troubles. Happily, the problems were all eventually ironed out and the class became a very useful component of the railway's stock.

All that was in the future, however, for Nos 60014 *Alexander Fleming* (front) and 60013 *Robert Boyle* as they wait to make their first marks on the main line. They were both named inside Brush Traction's factory in January. Although leaving the factory on this day, they were not formally accepted on to BR's books until 6 and 29 January 1993 respectively! *MJS*

**▼ 29 April**

Despite the rapid and widespread introduction of new classes and styles of DMUs from the early 1980s, many old units were still in regular squadron service. On this bright Sunday morning, Pressed Steel-built Class 117 unit L400 (with coach 51332 leading) restarts the 1010 Didcot-Oxford local service away from Radley station. Built in November 1959, 51332 just failed to celebrate its 40th birthday, being scrapped at MC Metal Processing's yard in Glasgow in April 1999. While fans of these older units grew in later years, the gathering of so many onlookers here is not for this train, however, but for the vision of No 71000 *Duke of Gloucester* steaming north on a steam special a few minutes later. *MJS*

Two more 'Brush 4s', seen five days and many miles apart.

### ▲ 14 May

After the withdrawal of Class 45s from the cross-country, Liverpool-York/Newcastle route in the late 1980s, the trains were taken over by the 47s, still retaining the space and comfort of loco-hauled coaches, rather than the more limited space within a DMU. Somewhat unusually double-headed, the 1325 Liverpool-Newcastle train drifts into Manchester (London Road) station behind Nos 47526 *Northumbria* (formerly D1109, built at Crewe in January 1967) and 47512 (formerly D1958, emerging from Brush one month later). Age plays little part in fortune, however, for while '526 was still nominally around into the 21st century, '512 succumbed to withdrawal from Crewe Diesel Depot in October 1991, after nearly a year in store. To the left, watched by a handful of waiting travellers, Chester-based two-car unit CH278 departs from Platform 3 in the opposite direction. *Tom Heavyside*

### ▼ 19 May

The presence of mail and parcels trains has diminished over the past couple of decades, to the extent that the sight of them is now very much rarer. Indeed, at the time of writing, Royal Mail had announced a cessation of TPOs and other mail trains in favour of road and air, and in the face of almost universal condemnation. In happier days, when Swindon still used its station parcels platform, No 47634 *Henry Ford* stands in the sidings to the east of the station, in blue livery with large numerals and BR's 'double-arrow' logo, having just arrived with this mixed rake of empties. Emerging from Brush in July 1964 as D1751, allocated to Landore depot, it became 47158 in February 1974 and its final persona on 21 December 1985. Having acquired the name at Dagenham Dock on 7 July 1981, recognising the links with the transporting of Ford cars by rail, it lost this honour in April 1991, preparatory to becoming *Holbeck* on 26 May of that year. *MJS*

▼ 21 May

Dalmuir station, on the north-western edge of Glasgow, has a very interesting layout, the result of competition between the North British and Caledonian companies for traffic along the northern banks of the River Clyde. This historic rivalry has produced what is, in effect, a glorified island station, but with the two main lines running independently on either side. This is the northern, ex-North British, side, from where, on the left, No 303085 waits to restart a westbound service, while 303010 leaves the bay platform 5, to make its way as the 1616 train right across the city to Motherwell. Introduced in July 1959 as Glasgow's 'Blue Trains', due to their striking Caledonian blue livery, the 91 Class 303 sets served the area well over the next 40-odd years, many surviving into 2003 against all the odds. Here, the units are in Strathclyde Transport's orange and black coat, but still looking attractive and remaining popular with the travelling public. Set 010 entered service in December 1959 and finally went into store at Shields depot in January 2001, whilst 085 was 13 months the younger and was one of the last sets to remain in traffic. The final curtain call was due at the end of December 2003. *Tom Heavyside*

▶ 23 May

Historically, the railways were invented and built primarily to move freight. The roads of the early 19th century were not ideal for moving loads of goods any great distances, and the alternatives were either long-winded or slow. The captains of industry embraced with open arms the improvements heralded by the coming of the railways, creating the society and sculpturing much of the countryside that we know today. The balance has now shifted, with the passenger being God on our modern railways, often to the detriment of both rail and our environment. Coal, however, has remained a major contributor to railway coffers, and rakes of wagons awaiting sorting and despatch can be seen in Toton north sidings as, on this bright late-spring day, No 47352, in the Engineer's all-over grey livery, is very much the exception as it hauls a ballast train past the Toton loco depot, on the extreme right. Built as D1833 at Brush in May 1965 and initially allocated to the Nottingham district, it spent much of its life in the Midlands area, becoming 47352 in March 1974. *Tom Heavyside*

▶ 26 May

The temptation for any railway photographer is to 'get up close', and indeed this is often successful, but there are many superb images to be had by not just stepping back, but by going further and placing the railway and its trains well into their landscape. The photographer has here used that premise to good effect at Grantshouse, skilfully utilising the five-barred gate as an element of scale, while capturing an unidentified HST as it heads south with the 1730 Edinburgh-King's Cross express. Some camera club judges would say that the gate should be open, to allow the eye to go through to the view, but the fact that it is here tight shut does not detract from the final effect with the rolling countryside and the precise positioning of the train overcoming this potential conflict. *Tom Heavyside*

**▼ 29 May**

The evening of Friday 26 January 1990 saw the old SE&CR Holborn Viaduct station abandoned after 116 years, in favour of a new facility close by, in connection with the enhanced cross-London 'Thameslink' service. Some of the aftermath of the 'destruction' can be seen in this view of No 319019 entering what was to become St Paul's Thameslink station, forming the 0850 Luton-Sevenoaks duty. Williams National House stands proudly in the background, atop what had previously been the concourse for Holborn Viaduct. As well as capturing the site in transition, the photographer has again shown his skill in placing the train in its context and providing a pleasing image. Built at York in January 1988 and used on the cross-London service from new, 019 was one of the sets refurbished at Wolverton Works in 1996, then assigned to the Victoria-Brighton 'Express' duties. *Brian Morrison*

**▶ 30 May**

The two Leicestershire sites of Vic Berry and Brush Traction provided images at the opposite ends of the railway spectrum. Partially screened by the results of the oxy-acetylene cutter, the final dismemberment of a 'Brush 4' – Class 47 – is well in hand at the Berry site, while in the background No 31259 (ironically a Brush loco), new as D5687 in February 1961 and withdrawn from Tinsley in March 1989, tops the pile of locos awaiting attention, with another Class 47 on the ground. Closer to the camera, coaches E70196 and E75253 from ER set 302280 support Provincial Sector-liveried Mk 1 Buffet M1554.

The Brush site suffered its share of unwanted attention during the Class 60 build, with too many inconsiderate individuals trespassing in their eagerness to see the latest examples. The man charged with the unenviable task of monitoring and challenging such 'visits' was Neville Mays. Rightly suspicious of those wanting access, Neville was, nevertheless, extremely courteous and accommodating for those he trusted. On the same day as the previous picture, he stands for his portrait among (l-r) Nos 60027 *Joseph Banks*, 60015 *Bow Fell*, 60016 *Langdale Pikes*, 60018 *Moel Siabod* and 60021 *Pen-y-Ghent*. Note how all of them are already fitted with their nameplates. Sadly, all of those pictured had lost these identities by 2002, although *Bow Fell* was still named as such when it became the first locomotive to wear the new Transrail livery on 14 July 1994. *Both MJS*

**30 May**

Parting is such sweet sorrow! A young man blows a kiss to his loved one, watched by the guard of 150150 as, with the doors all closed, the unit prepares to restart the 1249 Nottingham-Coventry service from Loughborough. Though having lost much of its magic with the ending of steam and the closure of the ex-Great Central line, which crossed these tracks on a bridge at the southern end of the station, beyond the road bridge seen here, this ex-Midland location still retains much of that railway's flavour. It was very special to my railway 'career', being where I started trainspotting in 1955 and where I recorded my first engine number. No 150150 is the last of the 150/1 two-car units, introduced from BREL York between October 1985 and March 1986, and benefits from not having the somewhat ugly corridor connection in the front-end design. *MJS*

**▲ 31 May**

Closely observed trains: the visit to Loughborough on the previous day was part of a trip with two friends to the North East. Having visited Immingham depot, we spent time on Ulceby station, watching the seemingly endless stream of freight trains to and from the docks. Here John Eales is on 'candid camera', blissfully unaware of the crew's interest, intent on capturing this double-headed consist on his video camera. 1964-vintage No 37225 and 37377, originally 37200 from late-1963 and here fitted with re-geared CP7 bogies, open the throttle and pick up speed after the curve, on a heavily laden westbound train. Note how the rake behind still leans on the curve.

**▼ 31 May**

Whilst Ulceby had a short, wooden platform with no waiting shelter, the nearby Brocklesby station was a much grander affair, displaying the sizeable but squat Junction signal box on the down platform and real architectural style in the main building. Sadly, the latter was closed on this day and forever shortly after! At the head of an empty 'merry-go-round' (mgr) train, No 56100, a mere eight and a half years old, is captured on film by a shirt-sleeved Paul Cleaver as it leads its rake towards the docks. The semaphore on the up line heralds the arrival of a Class 47-hauled freight a few seconds later. *Both MJS*

### 31 May

In the latter years of the 1990s, with the HSTs approaching their half-life renovations, thought was given to their future use and possible replacements. While one suggestion was running in shorter rakes than was then the norm, it is unlikely that even the most committed bean-counter could imagine trains this short – with passengers standing in the luggage compartments? Back to back, Nos 43069, in old-style 'InterCity 125' livery with nose-end power car number, and DVT-converted 43080, bearing the later, italicised 'InterCity' paintwork sans '125', power north through Doncaster station as, on the right, No 56073 approaches the platform road with yet another mgr train.

In more conventional style, No 43051, again with the number on the nose, trails the 1130 King's Cross-Glasgow express as it snakes out of Doncaster amidst a plethora of overhead wires, colour light signals and signs. My notes record that this was taken on my 'steam-driven' Canon AE1-P, with the Tamron 35-70mm zoom set at 65mm and the Ilford XP1 400ASA film used with a speed of 1/500 @ f11. The film was then processed locally under the one-hour system and viewed on the platform – the closest we could get to instant in those innocent pre-digital days! *Both MJS*

**31 May**

The final glimpse of that super weekend is at Rugby, on our way home. With the late afternoon sunshine casting attractive light patterns through the overall glass trainshed roof, No 86231 *Starlight Express*, substituting for a failed Class 90 and 'double-heading' with DVT 82143, slows for the stop, as intending passengers move forward on the wide platform. Built at Doncaster Works in November 1965 as E3126 in electric blue livery, it became 86231 under the TOPS programme in January 1974. Initially intended to become *Lady of the Lake*, actual naming to *Starlight Express* – linking it to the highly successful London stage show of the time – finally took place at Euston station on 1 November 1984. So much a feature of this photograph, the attractive overall roof was demolished and replaced – at great cost and against many opposing voices – in 2002, only for plans to be rethought for the station, which would necessitate the demolition of the new cover! *MJS*

**▲ 22 June**

Following their ousting from the Glasgow-Edinburgh push-pull duties, the specially converted Class 47s were shipped south, and the sudden appearance of Scotrail livery in the wilds of Oxfordshire was certainly a local talking-point and a must to see. At the head of a rake of Network SouthEast Mk 1/2a coaches, No 47715 *Haymarket* provides a variety of colour as it weaves its way out of Didcot station with the five-coach 1620 Paddington-Oxford commuter service. What travellers thought at the sight of 'Scotrail' on their train is unknown! The 47 had received its nameplates – not surprisingly – at Haymarket, on 24 August 1985, just five months after conversion from its previous identity, 47502. Originally D1945, from Brush in July 1966 as Works No 707, and allocated to the Nottingham district, *Haymarket* was withdrawn from Crewe Diesel Depot at the end of January 1999, but happily re-instated three years later, to become part of the Fragonset rail fleet. Note the

entrance to the Great Western Society preservation site to the left. *MJS*

**▼ 21 July**

As a variation of how many people you can squeeze into a Mini, hoards of passengers, luggage and backpacks pour out of No 143609 at Oxenholme. Summer skirts and tops, shorts and short-sleeved shirts mingle with the slightly fuller gear of the backpackers, many of whom are making their way to Platform 2 for their connection. This sudden invasion certainly has the attention of the three seated onlookers! Having just arrived at the main-line station as the 1000 service from Windermere, the unit is no doubt now a few inches higher having disgorged its load! Once again, the photographer has proved the old adage – include people in your picture. Without them, this shot would have been so much less successful. *Tom Heavyside*

**25 July**

So often, views of long-established railway centres betray what was, and how much more denuded are our railways today. With obvious signs of a wide expanse of track ripped up on the right, No 31463 departs from Rhyl with the four-coach 0944 Manchester Victoria-Llandudno train, the driver's arm nonchalantly resting on his open window. Within three months the former No 31297 had become 31563. With a 'sister' on the adjacent track, at least the shot still has the benefit of locomotives, a factor largely gone by the end of the decade; also, the signal box remains, to control the local semaphores, a presence now in a minority of locations after recent years of resignalling. The '209' milepost stands isolated in the waste ground to right of the leading coach.

A little later on the same day, the displacement of loco haulage mentioned above is evidenced by a 'Sprinter' Class 150, forming the 0926 Wakefield Westgate-Holyhead cross-country service. Class 158 units began driver-training between Chester and Holyhead on 28 February 1991. Ironically, on a much longer journey than that covered by 31463 above, the provision is a mere two coaches here, certainly providing a lot less space for holidaymakers. This delightful view across the tranquil waters of the River Conwy to the weather-stained castle, with just two heads 'above the parapet', once again exemplifies the value of placing the train in its landscape. *Both Tom Heavyside*

**▼ 25 July**

One of the economic saviours of the North Wales coastline has been the Penmaenmawr quarry, providing countless tons of ballast for both rail and road use – ironic, bearing in mind the rival A55 running alongside. Set between Conwy Bay, to the right, and Mynydd y Dref, it saw regular and frequent trains in the early 1990s, an example here being No 31158, in dull and uninteresting all-over grey garb, about to complete its shunting of the ancient and battered low-sided ballast wagons tailing out behind it. Introduced on the last day of 1959, 31158's first persona was as D5576 when it appeared from Brush in Loughborough. Its new TOPS number was acquired in February 1974. Following an initial allocation to 32A Norwich, it moved around the ex-GER area over the ensuing years before moving away when displaced by other locomotives. Would that the railway could have had some of the massive Government investment in the tarmac coursing around Penmaen-bach Point in the distance! *Tom Heavyside*

**▶ 5 August**

Unusual neighbours in an unusual setting: the first AC electrics to arrive at Vic Berry's yard in Leicester since the couple of Class 82s/83s in 1984/85, Nos 85019, its number repeated on the buffer beam, and 85025 stand next to 5ft 3in gauge CIE No 208 from Ireland, sat on a specially laid length of track. Withdrawn from Crewe Electric Depot on 1 December 1989 and recently arrived in the yard, the electrics caused quite a stir among the local enthusiasts. Introduced respectively on 5 December 1962 and 30 March 1963, as E3074 and E3080, they were two of a batch of 40 Class 85s built at Doncaster between August 1961 and December 1964. Sharing first-line WCML duties for a decade before being somewhat relegated by the introduction of Class 87s in the mid-1970s, the class continued to give excellent service up to the end in the early 1990s.

Across town, in the old Midland shed yard in Leicester, shunter No 08697 takes a breather between duties, overseen by that icon of the 1960s, Rowlatt's Hill high-rise flats behind. Despite the gradual reduction in diagrams and duties required of the depot over the past two decades, especially after the closure of the 'Leicester Gap', it resolutely refused to die, and even into the 21st century was providing home and shelter to both men and machines. Leicester (15C) first saw diesel shunters on 24 October 1959 and has been associated with them ever since. No 08697 was new from Horwich Works two months after that date, as D3864, going to 17A (Derby). It was moved a little around the Midlands area thereafter, being again a Derby (this time at Etches Park) engine by the turn of the century. *Both MJS*

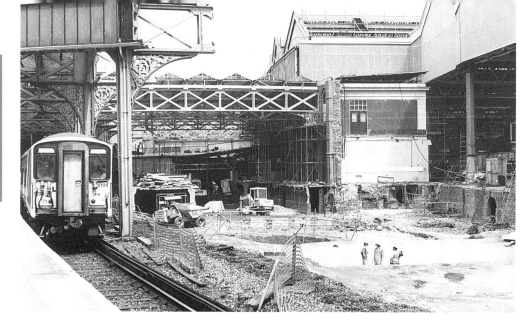

**▲ 6 August**

In a scene reminiscent of the destruction of Holborn Viaduct station seen on page 16, Waterloo here undergoes the same 'desecration' in preparation for the new Channel Tunnel international terminus on the west side of the station; begun in a ceremony at the site on 11 December 1990, it was finally completed in 1993. While the workmen consider their next moves in the foreground, hard hats, machines and plenty of rubble occupy the stripped-out 'cavern' on this western side of Waterloo. The double doors in the end wall, right of centre, now exposed, lead to a frightening drop! To the left, No 5724 clings to its traditional track, forming an unidentified service to Windsor & Eton Riverside. *Ray Ruffell*

**▼ 18 August**

Those who have been on or near the Cambrian Coast route will know of the magnificence of the scenery and the opportunities for attractive photography. Demonstrating the potential, with the train superbly placed within the picture, the photographer has here captured 1986-vintage Provincial Sector No 150134, running like a small caterpillar along a narrow ledge at the foot of the steep hillside, as it forms the 0800 Birmingham (New Street)-Pwllheli service at Abertafol, on the single-track route. Note how the sinuous curves of the coastal channels are mirrored by the course of the railway. *Brian Morrison*

## ▲ 21 August

We have already seen on page 24 some of the traffic provided to the railway by the Penmaenmawr quarry, with the Class 31 and its ancient rolling-stock. Heavier trains demanded more powerful traction, and here, coupled to wagons that most definitely improved the cost-benefit analysis, No 47445 leaves Llandudno Junction station with a ballast train bound for Manchester ARC. In the background, a 'sister' loco waits for the road with another freight. Introduced on 5 March 1964 from Crewe as D1561, its TOPS identity was assumed in November 1973. Originally an ER loco, at 41A (Darnall) shed in Sheffield, it remained an 'Eastern' engine for most of its relatively short life, although it is wearing a Crewe depot plaque in this shot, together with Speedlink Distribution decals. It was withdrawn from Tinsley depot (the replacement for the ex-steam shed at Darnall) on 24 June 1991. *Tom Heavyside*

## ▼ 24 August

For those south of the border, Scotland has always been a land of fascination, with both magnificent scenery and 'rare' motive power. That rareness is less pronounced with modern traction than it was in steam days, when locomotives did not wander the length and breadth of the land in the same way that they did at the close of the century, but for many, especially those collecting numbers or wishing to photograph motive power not seen 'at home', a trip north was *de rigueur*. Often the delights were of Class 37s on routine passenger trains, as here, with No 37128 as it arrives at Aberdeen with the 0815 from Inverness. Again nicely placed into the surrounding hinterland, the large bodyside logo and small snowploughs add to the excellently composed portrait, with the train perfectly framed by the buildings beyond and the quiet road and quaintly bricked property to the right. *Tom Heavyside*

## ▲ 6 September

With exhaust betraying effort and/or acceleration, No 47642 *Strathisla*, in Scotrail livery, heads the four-coach 0925 Stonehaven-Inverness train over the Forres Loop, just east of the station, nicely framed by semaphore and signpost placing us precisely on location. Note the somewhat denuded telegraph wires/posts on the left. No 47642 was originally D1621, new from Crewe on 19 September 1964 and allocated to 16A (Nottingham). In April 1966 it moved to the new 'Western Lines' Division, concurrent with the re-organisation of the Western Division depot codes with effect from the 23rd of that month. Becoming 47040 in March 1974, re-engineering saw it turn into 47624 exactly 12 years later, acquiring its name at Keith on 16 September 1986. This was removed in March 1992, to allow it to assume the *Resolute* mantle, as one of the new Res sector locomotives. It was again converted and renumbered on 9 March 1994, this time to 47766. *Tom Heavyside*

## ▼ 7 September

Effort of a different kind! Despite the many and far-reaching developments in our railway system over the past 150 years or so, there are still sections of line that hark back to the earliest days in requiring possession of a token to be allowed over a branch and/or single track. At Nairn, the driver of No 47541 *The Queen Mother*, at the head of the 1018 Elgin-Inverness train, has passed the relevant article to the signalman, having come off the single-line section, and prepares to continue his journey. Having wrapped the equipment around his shoulder, the signalman will return to his box, to relay the passage of the train to his colleague next along the route. Note his bike boldly parked against the attractive platform-based East box, used to speed between the two station signal boxes, situated at each end of the long platforms! Note also the interestingly styled ventilators on the roofs to the left of the box. *Tom Heavyside*

**▲ 7 September**

The two trains seen opposite were both bound for Inverness. Here we have the reverse – a train leaving that city. With its Scotrail livery – complete with Highland Stag motif – besmirched by a combination of dirt, oil and brake dust, No 47492 hardly lives up to its name of *The Enterprising Scot* as it leaves with the 1423 train to Aberdeen! To the left, No 08762 stands with coaching stock in the adjacent platform, its driver enjoying the sunshine on the bench? To the right, the ex-Inverness & Nairn Railway engine shed – later subsumed into Lochgorm Works – is still in use for diesels. Despite the grime, the judicious use of low light, tall chimneys and long shadows adds an attractive patina to the view. *Tom Heavyside*

**▲ 16 September**

At the other end of the country – indeed, in another country! – we find another Class 47, but one in a totally different condition. Like Scotland, Wales was in steam days a Mecca for enthusiasts as, again, engines plied their trade in many cases without even leaving, for example, the Valleys, let alone the country! Even into the 1980s there were cases of shunters that only worked locally, cut down for restricted clearances. Opened for the provision of servicing and light repairs for engines in the Swansea area, Landore here plays host to a very clean No 47530, seemingly far from home in its Network SouthEast livery, in for some remedial action. Yet another product of Brush, new as D1930 on 12 February 1966 and allocated to 82A (Bristol Bath Road), it was allocated the number 47253 under the TOPS renumbering, but this was aborted before it could be applied, the identity changing to 47530 in November 1973. *MJS*

### ◄ 16 September

We have seen the new generation of DMUs taking over from both their elder brethren and locomotives, but at this date what became known as the 'heritage' units were still around in some numbers. Again at Landore, one of Swansea's local units – denoted by the 'S' prefix to the 951 number – is 'Not To Be Moved' as a couple of fitters give total concentration to what should be done on an element of the driver's controls. Note the overhead haze caused by the unit's exhaust not finding a ready escape to the atmosphere!

The other large user of these older units in the southern half of the Principality was Cardiff. After the demise of steam and into the days of BR's 'Sectorisation', the part of the Canton steam shed standing on higher ground than its neighbour was given over to Regional Railways and its DMUs. Inside the servicing shed, C391 – proudly bearing the Welsh dragon and 'Valley Train' motif, but also betraying that it has been renumbered as a set from a previous identity – ticks over, also quietly polluting the atmosphere with its continual exhaust, at the head of a rake of four twin-car units. *Both MJS*

### ▲ 29 October

As the 20th century ended, St Pancras became the focus of attention and the location of major alterations to fit it to be a northern terminus of Channel Tunnel Eurostar trains. This would entail the provision of elongated platforms and, like Holborn Viaduct and Waterloo already seen, substantial amounts of rebuilding, including the removal of the landmark gasholders. All this is long in the future in this view, however, as No 47463 waits to leave with the 1N14 2255 Postal for Newcastle and 43197 leads the 2230 HST set bound for Derby. While the Class 47 went to its grave on 21 April 1995 un-

named and 'anonymous', 43197 acquired some fame as the flagship of *The Railway Magazine*. Then allocated to the north-south Virgin Cross Country pool, it was named *Railway Magazine Centenary 1897-1997* with due celebration at Plymouth station on 22 November 1996, witnessed by a clutch of staff, friends and supporters of the magazine. This recognition of longevity was removed in 2001, being rebranded simply *The Railway Magazine* at Neville Hill depot on 6 February. The low angle of this view, together with the attractive curved roof and artificial lighting, all contribute to a stunning portrait of the station temporarily asleep. *Brian Morrison*

### ▲ 5 November

One of the most radical developments on BR in the last decade and a half of its existence was the introduction of private operators, owning their own locomotives and running their own trains on the main line. Having seen the success enjoyed by Yeoman at Merehead, with stone trains from its quarry, ARC Whatley decided to join suit, and even imported the same basic style of US locomotive. As seen here, No 59104 – having arrived at Newport Docks from the General Motors plant in London, Ontario, less than a month previously and the first Class 59/1 to run in the UK – is captured passing the old Midland signal box at Saxby, with a Derby RTC test coach and Mk 3 sleeping cars while on the 0853 Derby-Cricklewood bogie test special. This was the day of its formal acceptance into the TOPS system by BR. It was subsequently named *Village of Great Elm* at Cambridge, of all places, during the Cambridge Gala Day event of 14 September 1991. *Colin Marsden*

### ▼ 8 November

The joint Railfreight Construction/Channel Tunnel-sponsored headboard says it all. Hauling the 1,000th Channel Tunnel segment train from TML's Isle of Grain Precast Concrete works to Shakespeare Cliff, Dover, Nos 33021 and 33051 *Shakespeare Cliff* double-head past High Halstow, on the Grain branch. An impressive achievement in less than three years of operation, like Penmaenmawr and its ballast this work has gone towards keeping this single-track branch open. The diagrams also kept the Class 33s alive probably longer than would otherwise have been the case, but ceased in mid-1991. Introduced on 14 January (as D6539) and 16 September 1961 (as D6569) respectively, both were initially allocated to 73C (Hither Green), a location that saw them as frequent visitors throughout their BR working lives. No 33021 was initially withdrawn from Stewarts Lane depot on 24 September 1996, but happily was resurrected one year later. The new century saw it still working, as another member of the Fragonset fleet. No 33051 was named at Isle of Grain on 16 May 1988 and also survived into the 21st century. *Brian Morrison*

# 1991

**10 February**

If quizzed, most of us would have to own to preferring to use our camera when the sun shone. However, impressive and atmospheric shots can be had in inclement weather, especially in black and white. Graphically illustrating the point is this view of No 33060 *Isle of Grain*, hauling 4CEP stock from London Victoria to Faversham with a '98' headcode, about to pass 2EPB No 6409 on an Orpington-Victoria local service, in the depths of winter. Pressed into service on many lines not normally seeing loco-hauled stock, the Class 33s came to the rescue of the EMUs severely affected by the heavy snowfalls. The dark tracks and third rails etched into the snow; the serried ranks of white rooftops and the cars and vans liberally covered with snow in the garden bottom left; the abandoned seesaw and relatively few footprints in the children's playground; the two intrepid swing-users pausing to watch the trains; and the luck of the two trains in exactly the right place, all add to the character of this superbly composed picture. *Brian Morrison*

**19 February**

Both night-time and pre-dawn can also be opportune periods for effective photography. In the latter category is this graphic illustration of 303088 standing by the impressive hydraulic buffer stops at Glasgow Central, waiting to become the 0650 to Neilston. Perhaps not surprisingly, the platforms are empty! The excellent use of the available lighting, the delineation of the roof truss tracery and side 'window arches' and the telling inclusion of those buffer stops in the foreground, all pointing to a common point on the horizon, make for an evocative and successful portrait. Another of Glasgow's 'Blue Trains', 303088's three-car set entered service in February 1961, the youngest bar three of the 91 sets built at the nearby Linwood Works, Paisley, of Pressed Steel Ltd. It was also one of the last sets to survive. The three cars comprised a Driver Trailer Second (DTS – 75798), a Motor Brake Second (MBS – 68164) and a Battery Driving Trailer Second (BDTS – 75854). *Brian Morrison*

**24 February**

We have already seen the Class 60s at their birthplace, where many were held while the teething troubles were remedied. Once solved, however, the locomotives were soon cascaded to the various points of our railway compass. By this date, No 60008 *Moel Fammau*, still displaying its newness, stands outside what was left of covered accommodation at Westbury depot, between route-learning duties for the class on local stone trains. Interestingly, due to the aforementioned early problems, 60008 was not officially accepted into BR's stock until 11 December 1992 – two years after it started work!

Although the class was originally allocated a unified set of names, depicting sights of awe and wonder in and personalities of the UK, after No 1 was emblazoned as *Steadfast*, Privatisation saw an unseemly haste to remove many of them, often to be replaced by appendages of dubious quality and/or relevance. No 60008 lost its name in September 1995, to assume the questionable honour of becoming *Gypsum Queen II* at Kirby Thore on the 27th of the month. As quickly as the name vanished, so did this site at Westbury, together with the buildings, as stabling and servicing moved elsewhere. *MJS*

**▲ 13 March**

Visions of two London termini. By this time in 1991, the long service on the Southern Region of BR by Class 50s was approaching its twilight years. Many of their erstwhile duties had already been wrenched away and the Waterloo-Exeter semi-fasts were their sole remaining stronghold. With the writing well and truly on the wall, No 50031 *Hood*, whose bodywork on this day had most certainly seen better times, waits under Waterloo's skeletal roof at 1457 at the head of its rake of Mk IIs, forming the 1515 to Exeter. The shadows cast by the angle of the lowering late-winter sun seem to pick out a sad expression on the locomotive's 'face'. At the far end, at the buffers, stands 'sister' No 50037 *Illustrious*, which had brought the previous inwards train from the West Country. Before the onset of rush-hour, note how few humans are discernible – just one! *MJS*

**▼ 13 March**

Across London earlier in the day, Paddington's platforms are home to twice as many people and full of trains, with HSTs – Nos 43026 *City of Westminster*, very recently re-united with its nameplates of 1985, and 43141 predominant – and Nos 47701 and 47598 all waiting for their 'right away'. Another ex-Scottish push-pull converted machine, 47701 had lost its *Saint Andrew* plates five months earlier; it would become *Old Oak Common Traction & Rolling Stock Depot* five months after this view. Formerly 47182, '598 was to be converted to 47742 on 14 June 1995. Not always an easy station to capture successfully, the *contre jour* early morning lighting here makes for an appealing canvas of light and shade. A lone spotter waits to collect numbers, while the inherent pollution of diesel engines ticking over is well seen in the exhausts. *MJS*

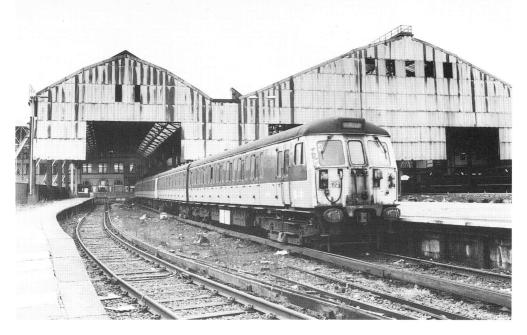

### 19 March

Visions of two Manchester termini. During the 1990s the long-standing Manchester-Bury third-rail electric services were displaced by the new Metro system, with most of the old units despatched for scrapping. This view, not long before the closure of most of the route to heavy rail on 16 August, with grass and rubbish liberally strewn between the tracks, and the rather careworn frontage to the unit echoing the dilapidated state of the trainshed, is a graphic illustration of a run-down situation and one requiring investment and new ideas. Standing in the side terminal platform at Victoria station, the four-car train, comprising M65458, M77179, M65451 and M77172, waits to form the 1030 Metro service to Bury.

While some progress has been for the benefit of customers, including up-dated facilities, much of the switch from loco-hauled trains to DMUs during our period has been more for the economics of the rail industry than for the comfort of the travelling public. Thus, unit 155330, seen standing in Platform 6 at Piccadilly station, rather than being a modernised local service, is the provision given for the 1200 Cross-Country train to Cardiff Central! With cramped internal conditions and window pillars not always being conducive to viewing the passing scenery, it was definitely not state-of-the-art. Nearly an hour before departure time, there is, not surprisingly, no rush for seats! Introduced in April 1988, this Leyland DMS+DMSL two-car unit was summarily split with the rethink of certain service needs, with its two coaches becoming Nos 153330 (52330) and 153380 (57330). *Both MJS*

### ▲ 3 April

In direct comparison to the view and comments of the picture of 155330 on the previous page, Topsham, on the Exmouth branch, is here being given a more lavish provision. To the right, Derby Works Class 108 DMCL 52053, from set 905, waits for access to the single track ahead with the 1745 Exmouth-Paignton duty, whilst set 967 approaches with the 1748 Exeter Central-Exmouth local service – three coaches for such a short trip, as opposed to the two-car Cross Country train from Manchester Victoria! Just short of 18 months later, 52053 was withdrawn from capital stock, to become a Sandite/route-learning coach as Departmental 977807, based at Longsight TMD; it was condemned prior to the close of 1993. Interestingly, the level crossing box has a 'VISA' sticker in the window! *Tom Heavyside*

### ▼ 4 April

The following day we are in Cornwall. The weedkilling train travelled far and wide throughout the system, spraying its cocktail of noxious chemicals and taking its sleeping accommodation with it. For the casual observer, it was a surprise to meet up with the train and, photographically, a delight to be able to snap 'something different'. Nicely framed by the ex-GWR lower-quadrant semaphores, No 20901 *Nancy* heads the train into the yard at Lostwithiel, having completed its duties on the Fowey branch. No 20904 *Janis*, out of sight here, brings up the rear – the two locos are provided to prevent the necessity of running-round at termini. No 20901 was converted from 20041, and '904 from 20101, both on 29 March 1989, being based in their new guises in or around the Cumbria area. Note the signage, advising a cautious speed limit around the curve and the stopping point for nine-car HSTs. *Tom Heavyside*

## ▲ 6 April

Once more illustrating the effectiveness of black and white film to capture images of real quality in adverse conditions, the reflections on the sodden platform from the heavy rain here add to the effect, as No 50031 *Hood* is once again seen, in large bodyside number and logo livery, this time at the other end of its regular run, at Exeter Central. The engines purr in Platform 3 as it waits to start its run to London Waterloo as the 1422 from Exeter St David's. Two hapless passengers wait under the shelter, no doubt wondering what this mad photographer is up to! To the right, a solitary siding clings to the railway land. *Tom Heavyside*

## ▼ 9 April

Like the weedkilling trains, snapping an unscheduled test train was a boon to the railway photographer. In completely contrasting conditions to the above, one such, the Derby RTC special Track Recording Train, is here seen heading under Fenchurch Street station signal box, heading for Shoeburyness, with *Laboratory 5* at the head of the consist. Similarly topped-and-tailed, however, No 31135 heads the rake, while 31224 brings up the rear. Note how the slightly low angle and early spring side-lighting accentuate the image, to its benefit, highlighting the details of the locomotive and picking out the overhead wires, especially against the dark bulk of the box. New to 32B (Ipswich) on 24 September 1959, as D5553, 31135 succumbed to a declining need for its services on 14 January 2000, whereas 31224, emerging from Brush a year later to go to 34G (Finsbury Park), was still in service at the time of writing as a Fragonset locomotive. *Brian Morrison*

### 13 April

The influx of Class 60s on to the freight scene, with their power in hauling long and heavy trains, sounded the final death knell for the ageing Class 20s, which so often had been used in tandem to achieve the necessary power output. Old and new are juxtaposed in this view inside Toton shed, where No 60032 *William Booth* (centre) had been allocated for crew training. To the left stand Nos 20085 and 20173 with two brethren, while to the right two types that were introduced by BR in the 1970s and '80s are represented by Nos 56123 *Drax Power Station* and 58032. Built between 1984 and 1987, the Class 58s have not been a good economic investment, despite their modular design and hopes for the future; 58032, new in August 1985, was withdrawn in

January 2000, by then in Mainline blue livery and having accumulated a mere 8,422 hours of running. Note how the judicious – and as found! – positioning of the two mobile ladder platforms, the regular roof light pattern and the line of perspective all combine to make a more dynamic picture.

Moving north from Toton, night has fallen, but the railway is not asleep! With the artificial light picking out the attractive motif in the platform canopies' supporting brackets, 'Metro Train' unit 144022, having lost its '1' numeral, stands at the head of a five-car rake at Skipton. The three-car unit was introduced in June 1987, but like its companions it was not heralded by travellers as an unmitigated success! Once again, having the camera ready at night provides an image that would have been just ordinary in daylight. *Both MJS*

## 14 April

It was a truism in steam days – when to a degree railway photography was easier, with the smoke and steam adding their own vital ingredients – that you have to have an eye for the more unusual angle, location, vantage point, light conditions, etc, but that is even more so to create modern railway photography. Here the use of the shed doorway at Tinsley shed, the framing of the fuel stage, the vertical format and the contrast between sunshine and shade has composed a pleasing view of Nos 47241 and 08434 in the shed yard, seen past the cab of 47313. Even the dirt on the raised platform is picked out and adds to the overall atmosphere. No 47241, here with roof panels open for attention, was named *The Silcock Express* at Tinsley on 3 August 1994, only for the name to be replaced by *Halewood Silver Jubilee* on 12 September 1995, again at Tinsley. At the date of this photograph, 47313 bore the unofficial name of *Curlew*. Its was withdrawn on 19 January 1999, only to be re-instated in March 2002, to join the expanding Fragonset fleet. The Class 08 was also named on this date, assuming an unofficial *Midland* name at the depot on 27 October 1987; it was culled from capital stock in February 1992.

The second shed shot on the same day again utilises the available bright side-light and surrounding infrastructure to frame and compose the image, rather than just produce a front-three-quarter portrait of the locomotives. 1980-vintage No 56081 stands in the shed yard at Knottingley with 'sister' 56076, of a similar age, enjoying the warm spring sunshine. On this day, apart from the odd shunter, Class 56s dominated the depot. *Both MJS*

**25 April**

As if to exemplify the comments already made on composition and the use of the surroundings, the photographer has here stood well back, placing the train in its context and adding human interest on the beach. A couple of families do their best to enjoy what looks to be a windswept stretch of sand, at a location that is often snapped from a totally different angle. Long before the 'coats of many colours' adorned this motive power, HST power cars Nos 43073 and 43054 wear the latest 'InterCity' derivative as they top-and-tail a return Workington-St Pancras excursion across Arnside Viaduct, a wisp of exhaust from the latter betraying acceleration. This was thought to be the first visit of an HST to this line, and interestingly, despite the plethora of names bestowed on HST power cars, neither of these two (new in 1978 and 1977 respectively) has been so blessed at the time of writing. *Tom Heavyside*

Two final views of Vic Berry's scrapyard.

## ▲ 1 January: before…

At the beginning of the year, piles of coaches (18 visible in this picture alone!) and locomotives still littered Vic's yard in Leicester as evidenced here by the half-dismembered bodies of Nos 33015 (top), 33017 and 25213, summarily dumped awaiting their turn for cutting. The two 33s were new from Birmingham Railway & Carriage Company, as D6523 on 24 September and D6526 on 15 October 1960 respectively, travelling to 73C (Hither Green), where all other members of the class, both before and after, were initially allocated. As a class of 98 examples, they replaced an even greater number of ageing steam locomotives in the South East of England, and over the years travelled to many parts well away from this area. Finally withdrawn from Eastleigh depot, they departed in July 1989 and January 1988. By comparison, No 25213 started life on 12 November 1965 as D7563, one of 478

Class 24/25s developed over a nine-year period. Initial allocation was the Nottingham area, but it was finally withdrawn from Crewe Diesel Depot on 19 March 1987, but not before it had carried *Castell y Waun/Chirk Castle* nameplates. *MJS*

## ▼ 12 May: …after

In the early hours of Sunday 10 March the yard and its contents became a blazing inferno, when much of the stacked coaching stock caught fire. The alarm was raised at 0412, and soon afterwards clouds of thick, acrid black smoke filled the Leicester sky, giving rise to fears of asbestos contamination and bringing the highly focused attention of both press and authorities to the yard. The end result was the closure of the operation. Some of the aftermath is seen in this view, with the ex-SR EMU power car, lower left, barely recognisable. Judging by the twisted metal, one can only guess at the temperatures that must have been generated at the fire's height! *MJS*

### ▲ 20 May

A picture that is a delight on many fronts; and definitely a case of two heads being better than one, as twin Brush Type 2s Nos 31327 and 31329 head into Castleford station with a Rylestone-Hull Tilcon stone train. With stormy clouds in the distance, the long rake snakes past the attractive, unspoilt semaphore gantries and the still-functioning Station signal box. Perhaps celebrating its position as the last Brush 2 built – as D5862 in October 1962 – No 31327 here bears a unique livery of large bodyside logo and numerals but with the addition of full number on the front solebar. Named *Phillips-Imperial* on 27 May 1987 at Port Clarence, Teeside, it was again anonymous by the time of this view, losing the plates in September 1990. Note on the right, beyond the substantial brick wall, yet another car park occupying former railway land. *Tom Heavyside*

### ▼ 20 May

Enjoying the sunshine of the same day, but with a shorter rake, is No 37506, manoeuvring from the 'main line' straight ahead and heading south on the ex-NER route to Ferrybridge, hauling a Tees-Tinsley scrap train past South Milford Junction. The inclusion of the snaking crossovers adds to the overall appeal. One of the earliest EE Type 3s built, as D6707 on 3 February 1961, it became No 37007 exactly 13 years later, then 37506 on 3 April 1986. Still displaying the position of the original nose-end doors, it was named *British Steel Skinningrove* at Thornaby in March 1987. The nameplates were removed in September 1994, followed by another renumbering on 20 April 1995, to 37604, for Channel Tunnel work. *Tom Heavyside*

### ▲ 20 May

On the same day as the picture on the previous page, but this time in London, the bright sunshine is not so evident, but does serve to enhance the available light in the suburban platforms of King's Cross station in this photograph of members of the same class, but with different front ends. With less than 2 minutes to go, 317344 waits to be the 1115 to Cambridge, while on the right 317353 is empty stock, not due to work until later in the afternoon. Initially built as one of 48 units for service on the newly electrified St Pancras/Moorgate-Bedford route, they were displaced by 319s in 1987. Thirty-five of the clutch went to Bletchley for the Euston-Bletchley/Milton Keynes stretch, while the rest went to Hornsey, where they joined 24 later kin with improved front-ends, for service out of King's Cross. The 35 were again ousted from their duties, by 321s this time, in 1989, at which juncture they joined the rest of the fleet on the runs to Cambridge/Peterborough. No 317344 was new in December 1982, the more cleanly designed '353 in January 1986. *MJS*

### ▶ 22 May

While what became known as the 'Thames Turbos' were making their presence felt in the Network SouthEast routes out of Paddington and Marylebone, the 'heritage' units were still hanging on, but by this date the leading Class 101 three-car unit L840 in blue and grey – comprising 53311 (new as 50311), 59117, and 53322 (formerly 50322), all new in February 1958 – was very much a rarity. It is here coupled to single-car L125 in Network SouthEast livery (55025, new in October 1960 and later Sandite Departmental 977859), forming the 1330 Reading-Banbury service, slowing for the Heyford stop. The Oxford Canal is just beyond the trees on the left. *MJS*

**23 May**

We have already seen the weedkilling train at Lostwithiel; it has now travelled to Kent and is seen passing the site of Lydd Town station, closed on 3 January 1966. Note that in this isolated location the station building is still largely intact. The low, flat landscape towards Brookland is clear from this angle. As the signalman attends to the Lydd Town level crossing gates, the driver of No 20901 *Nancy* prepares to move forward with the 0920 Hither Green-Ashford via Dungeness and Margate working. *Brian Morrison*

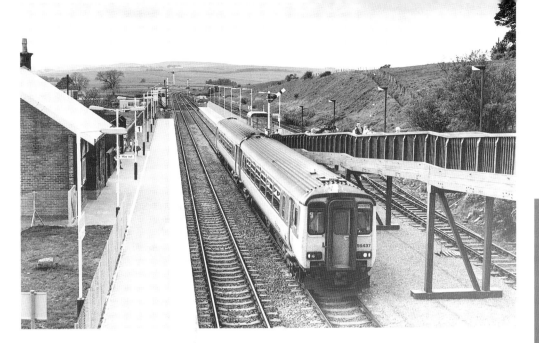

## ▲ 27 May

After the introduction and success of the Class 150 'Sprinter' DMUs, other types appeared, incorporating lessons learned from those earlier sets, as well as being designed for other, often long-range duties. One such is No 156437, bearing the 'Sprinter' branding that was later abandoned, restarting the 1548 Glasgow-Newcastle service from New Cumnock on the new station's opening day. The slightly staggered platforms are pristine and seemingly a little incongruous with the semaphores and ex-G&SWR signal box. The original station closed to passengers on 6 December 1965, but freight presumably played an important part in the locality, judging by the retention of the sidings on the right. The first Class 156 appeared from Metropolitan Cammell in November 1987 and was quickly on test. The build followed in steady order, with '437 coming on stream the following August. *Tom Heavyside*

## ▼ 8 June

With steam specials increasingly allowed during our last years of BR, No 48151 began regular outings, to the delight of fans and photographers alike. Though constructed as a freight engine, at Crewe in 1942 ready for the war effort, the loco is equally at home with passenger duties and certainly looks the part as it crosses Levens Viaduct, near Ulverston, with 'The Furness Flyer', a Carnforth-Barrow shuttle. It was withdrawn in January 1968 from 8E (Northwich) shed, but not before a star had been placed under the number on the cabside, denoting the balancing of the wheels, facilitating faster running – note that it still bears the mark. *Tom Heavyside*

**26 June**

Oops! Consternation and consideration near Chislehurst, as the various bodies ponder precisely how best to re-rail No 59104, which has decided on a detour while hauling the 2055 stone train from Whatley to Chislehurst. No 33033 stands by, ready to give any necessary assistance with the re-railing train, at the same time shielding the unfortunate spectacle from the passengers of the 1032 Orpington-Charing Cross local service, the rear of which is formed of 4EPB 5606. No doubt there were conflicting views on the pros and cons of the situation! *Brian Morrison*

### ▶ 28 June

As already mentioned, parcels and mail trains suffered reductions in traffic and rosters during the 1990s, wiping trains and sights such as this from the system. In slightly happier times, No 31290 stands with a multifarious mix of coach types and liveries at Bolton, the driver patiently waiting for the road. Increasingly to become an arch rival for some of the business, two Royal Mail vans stand to the right, having disgorged their contents on to this train. Bucking many a trend, however, Bolton's Parcels Depot once more became a hive of activity in 1990, after many years of decline, following the transfer of many services that had previously originated at Manchester Piccadilly. Fresh from Brush on 9 November 1961, No 31290 was originally D5822, receiving its TOPS number in February 1974. Its first allocation was to 41A (Darnall) and it stayed an ER machine for many years, before finding its way to more westerly routes and finally being withdrawn from Toton depot on 24 September 1996. Note the interesting architecture beyond, some evidencing a history of wealth in the town. *Tom Heavyside*

### ▶ 4 July

Some of the more obscure branches/ lines and traffic also disappeared during the period – some were closed and abandoned, some mothballed for possible future use. In glorious summer sunshine Nos 20066, complete with original headcode discs, and 20137 *Murray B Hofmeyer* head along the since-closed Cameron Bridge branch in Scotland, with a short rake of just four tanks bound for Thornton yard. The lens foreshortening heightens the effect of the pitched roofs. *Brian Morrison*

### ▶ 5 July

Another day, and another branch since closed: this time it is the Auchtermuchty branch that has ceased feeding Thornton yard, ending InterCity-liveried No 08761's opportunities of hauling 'Tullis Russel' hoppers over the metals. Passenger services ceased as early as 5 June 1950 over the whole branch, but freight survived until 5 October 1964 west of Auchtermuchty, leaving just the short stub seen here to the junction at Ladybank. Judging by the state of the track and the

surrounding undergrowth, not many trains were running at the date of this view! *Brian Morrison*

### 7 July

Selhurst depot, in deepest Surrey, was split during the latter years of BR into two specific facilities – Level 4 and Level 5. In the latter, capable of heavier maintenance and repairs than its neighbour, 489 GLV No 9104's body rests on stands, releasing the bogies for examination in an attempt to identify the cause of rough riding.

Across the northern reaches of Kent, at Slade Green depot, a phalanx of EMUs stands beneath the footbridge, 'under starter's orders'. Left to right are examples of a variety of classes – 5124, 5264, 5502, 3304 and 6417. This variety was not to last too long, however, with the arrival of Class 465 'Networker' units from 1 April 1992.

Out on the road, yet another type curves under the magnificent ex-SR 1923 Canterbury West signal box, about to enter the station of that name with the 0915 Ramsgate-Charing Cross service. The box became a listed building during the 1990s. No 1613, one of the Class 411 4CEP EMUs built for the Kent Coast electrification from 1958, is here running some 9 minutes late on this service. The Connex fleet of these has now been withdrawn, but examples are still extant with South West Trains. *All MJS*

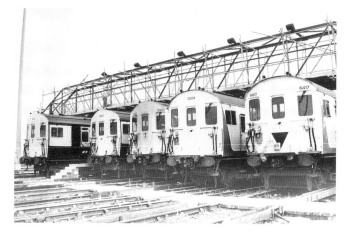

**▲ 15 July**
The spread of long-distance DMUs has now radiated to the outer reaches of the Scottish system. A group of seven young walkers are closely watched by the guard at Ardlui, as they alight from No 156493, running as the 0812 Glasgow (Queen Street)-Oban service. To the left, a six-car train, made up of three two-car sets, with 156436 trailing, heads in the opposite direction. *Ray Ruffell*

**▼ 16 July**
Another parcels train: this one is passing at speed through the delightful ex-Midland station at Melton Mowbray, behind all-blue No 31425. Built as D5804 on 29 June 1961, yet another Brush Type 2 initially allocated to 41A (Darnall), its first TOPS number, assumed in March 1974, was 31274. A withdrawal from service came at Thornaby on 5 October 1980, but this was reprieved on 27 March 1983, following which it became 31425 on 30 September. The end came less than five months after this shot, at Crewe Diesel Depot on 5 December 1991. Note the wealth of original architecture still present at this venue, thankfully having avoided desecration in the name of progress. Pictured at 1732, the long shadows betray the shortening days as the summer solstice has passed. *MJS*

**30 July**

In the first of two views of 'heritage' DMUs still managing to ply their trade along and around the North Wales coast line, LO601 pauses at Llandudno Junction station, which serves both the Conwy Valley line and the 3-mile stretch to Llandudno, as the 0936 Blaenau Ffestiniog-Llandudno local. Some shoppers and flexi-time commuters have detrained, while other passengers scurry to climb aboard, the events closely watched by the driver from his window. Not a place of great architectural merit, at the least the solid lift pillars and the covered footbridge, together with the inclusion of the human element, with doors being held open, turn an otherwise 'bog-standard' picture into one of far greater interest and satisfaction.

Later in the day, another Longsight-based unit – denoted by the 'LO' prefix to the set number – LO287 (with coach 54203 leading) waits to leave Llandudno as the 1413 service to Manchester Victoria. The guard checks the platform for late-comers from his open door, while the driver watches both the photographer and the weather as time approaches for departure – seconds after this shot was taken, the heavens opened! As so often in today's railway, there is evidence of what once was: blocked-off entrances, supports no longer holding trainshed roofs, bricked-up doorways and windows – all in evidence at the station on this day. The station's overall roof was demolished during 1990. *Both MJS*

### ▲ 16 August

We have already seen the Class 504 units eking out their days on the Manchester Victoria-Bury route, the shot on page 37 being at one end of the line. This is the view at Bury on the very last day of heavy rail. On the left, No 504456, with DMBSO 77177 leading, forms the 1300 service to Crumpsall, while 504445, with 77166 at the front, is here stabled in Platform 2 as a spare unit, in case of need. *Brian Morrison*

### ▼ 21 August

Yet another example of how to make an interesting picture out of superficially uninspiring ingredients. Approaching one of the many crew-operated manual level crossings on the line,

No 60050 *Roseberry Topping* slows for the one at Ainderby Steeple, on the ex-NER Northallerton-Hawes branch, while hauling the daily Tees Yard-Redmire train of limestone hoppers. *Roseberry* only emerged from Brush on 8 March, but its 'newness' is hard to appreciate in these dull conditions! Named before leaving the factory, it become anonymous in October 1996. The crew rest awhile, waiting for the gates to be opened; no doubt the engine, too, is glad of a respite in view of length of the consist behind it. Note the ageing concrete posts, gently rotting sleepers and the somewhat ad hoc netting on the gates. The hand-scrawled message on the cross-member – just discernible above the loco – exhorts all to 'Lock these gates'! *Brian Morrison*

**28 August**
Once more, the strategic placing of the train within its landscape makes for a very pleasing image. Viewed from the Highland Wildlife Farm at Craig, with the sun high in the sky, No 37232 *The Institution of Railway Signal Engineers* crosses the shallow man-made embankment skirting Loch Carron on the West Highland line, as it heads west with the 1227 Inverness-Kyle of Lochalsh service. A young couple, bottom right, watch the train pass the tiny inlet, which, although holding a boat, does not look to have seen water in the very recent past! New as D6932 in March 1964 and renumbered exactly ten years later, the Class 37 was denuded of its nameplates in 1999. *Tom Heavyside*

**29 August**
The following day, we have reached the terminus at Kyle of Lochalsh, magical to many as well as Michael Palin! The weather is still good, but the slightly later time of day is displayed in the longer shadows cast by No 37409 *Loch Awe*. Note the bold non-standard positioning of '409' on the engine's nose, and the observation car immediately behind the locomotive, in green and white livery, and the Gaelic and English 'Welcome to the Highlands' sign. The Class 37 has a six-coach rake for its journey across Scotland, as the 1505 to Inverness, compared to 37232 above. *Tom Heavyside*

**29 August**
The return journey, north-eastwards from Kyle, has begun and our pause is to witness No 37156 easing its four-coach load past Badicaul in the lowering sun, forming the 1705 service to Inverness. Once more, placing the gently curving train as 'head-on', rather than the more traditional 'front-three-quarter', has enhanced the impact and made for a more pleasing image. *Tom Heavyside*

**9 September**

One of the most popular steam engines back on the main line during our timescale, certainly in the southern half of the country, was 'King' Class No 6024 *King Edward I*. Normal views show it pounding along the permanent way, through attractive countryside, with smoke (hopefully white!) streaming gracefully behind, but this time it is captured 'back home' in Swindon, its place of birth. Sadly here graced with a hideously painted support coach, it clearly exemplifies why the

GWR locomotives were so beloved of enthusiasts, especially these mighty engines. Designed by Collett and new from Swindon in 1930, as one of a class of 30 of the most powerful passenger locomotives in the country, it ended its British Railways working life in June 1962, allocated to Cardiff (Canton) shed. Happily restored to main-line condition, it is normally based at the GWS centre in Swindon. Note the original Brunel-inspired buildings beyond the locomotive, now occupied by the archives of the National Monuments Records Office. *MJS*

**1991**

**▼ 10 September**

Emerging into the bright sunshine from the more gloomy depths of Waterloo station, No 50030 *Repulse* is here still valiantly clinging to its London-West Country duties, but the end is moving ever closer. On this day it is preparing to cross over to the tracks seen to its left, to nudge up to the coaching stock seen on the extreme right to become the 1100 semi-fast service to Exeter (St David's). Withdrawal came a little over six months later, from Laira depot on 8 April 1992. Originally built at English Electric's Vulcan Foundry for duties on the WCML as D430 on 25 June 1968, it was transferred, together with other class members, to the WR when displaced by the completion of electrification on the Euston-Glasgow route. Named after a battleship, like the others, it became *Repulse* at Laira on 10 April 1978. *MJS*

**▼ 10 September**

A location visited by thousands of commuters weekly, but very much more rarely by photographers: at the time, however, it could have been a regular destination for many enthusiasts, being the headquarters of publisher Ian Allan, and workplace of the late-lamented Handel Kardas, then editor of *Railway World*. No 5911 stands at Shepperton, the terminus of the branch from Strawberry Hill, after bringing passengers to the town as the 1509 service from Waterloo. Note the bikes of some of those commuters. *MJS*

**13 October**

An innocuous enough scene on the face of it, but all is not what it appears! For this is not the WCML out of Euston, but its near neighbour, the ex-Midland St Pancras main line! At the time of writing, No 87001 has just received a repaint into its original all-over blue, to both recognise its 30th year of service and to give it a special mantle to wear in its final months of front-line service. It has also been re-acquainted with its *Stephenson* name, with which it was graced from January 1976 to October the following year, when the honour was bestowed upon 87101.

Back in 1991, however, it is seen (right) bearing another famous name – *Royal Scot* – on this unfamiliar territory. With an engineer's occupation under way near Wembley, services from Liverpool and Holyhead were diverted to this route and 87001 is seen here propelling the 1035 St Pancras-Liverpool (Lime Street) train away from the capital, past Nos 90008 *The Birmingham Royal Ballet* – acting as stand-by – 56063 *Bardon Hill* and 47539 *Rochdale Pioneers*. This is thought to be the first visit to this line by both Class 90 and 87 locos. *Brian Morrison*

# 1992

**14 January**

Buxton is one of the highest towns in England and, as the saying goes, if it snows anywhere it snows in Buxton – it thus makes sense to be good railway Scouts and 'be prepared'! Hence the provision in Buxton station on this January night of twin-ended full-height snowploughs, powered mid-way by two Class 31s. In this superbly photographed view, which – presumably with the aid of a tripod – gives pin-sharp definition and impressive depth of field, Nos 31178 and 31238 are sandwiched between ADB 965226 and ADB 965222. The far-end fan window nicely frames the 156 unit waiting in Platform 2, and the starburst lighting effects give the finishing touch. Both locomotives were of 1960 vintage, appearing from Brush respectively on 17 March – as D5599 to 34B (Hornsey) – and 10 November – as D5665 to 31B (March). *Colin Marsden*

## ▲ 5 February

Another night and another brightly lit but empty platform awaiting custom, this time showing an early visit on normal duties of a 'Turbo' to High Wycombe. The equally illuminated cab, together with the even brighter digital 'Marylebone via Gerrards Cross' destination display, all add to the appeal of No 165012, still clean from day-to-day grime, standing as empty stock in the bay Platform 1 – later to be a service to Marylebone. Barely three months old, having emerged from BREL York in the previous November, the Class 165 outwardly gave the impression of a step-up in quality over the older units it replaced, and this was echoed in the very positive passenger reactions. Note that the angle of the slabs leading to the ghostly solitary figure at the far end does not mirror the platform edging. *MJS*

## ▼ 14 February

Many highly attractive photographs are taken out in the countryside, where beautiful surroundings add to the overall attraction, but industrial settings can also provide equally appealing images, albeit of a wholly different aesthetic. In this 'grubby' hinterland No 60045 *Josephine Butler* threads its path through the giant Lever Brothers complex at Warrington, slowly shifting a return mgr from Fiddler's Ferry to Parkside Colliery past semaphores and Crosfields Crossing box. Less than a year old, the grime of its freight duties is showing on the bodyside of the Class 60. The nameplates were fitted at Brush before delivery and were removed in 1997, prior to the locomotive being renamed *The Permanent Way Institution* at Toton on 8 November of that year. *Brian Morrison*

**1992**

## ▲ 16 March

Over the years there have been many innovations on our railways, some highly successful, others not so, despite, in many cases, having genuine merit. One of the latter cases was the introduction of the 'Piggyback' container system by Charterail. This enabled goods to be transhipped between rail and road traction relatively easily and within tight space constraints, enhancing the effectiveness of rail-to-road competition by the road trailer being able to drive away with its load the relatively short distance from railhead to customer. Petfoods in Melton Mowbray was one of the first companies to use the system (opened on 12 November 1991 by Transport Secretary Malcolm Rifkind) to apparently good effect, and the road journey was indeed very short – a matter of a couple of hundred yards! Sadly, the optimism was not to bear fruit and the operation was ended on 27 August, the result of price competition from road! In this view No 08597, apparently working 'wrong line', manoeuvres the rake of special wagons into Melton station before routing them into Petfoods' sidings out of shot to the left of picture. The wisp of exhaust betrays the shunter's efforts, all captured on video (left). *MJS*

## ▼ 16 March

Post-Privatisation, the ex-BR Works complexes have seen much change, either from changes in thinking or outside contractors/TOCs taking on the provision of need themselves. Some have been threatened with closure and others have seen a diminution in their overall workload. The ex-LNER Works at Doncaster has had both elements thrust on it as a 'double whammy' and has clung on seemingly by a thread. In somewhat happier times, when locomotives were still needed in numbers, Nos 47306, unofficially named *Goshawk*, and 47310 *Raven* – equally unofficially – are raised from their bogies in No 2 Bay of 'The Plant', undergoing their respective exams. Both appearing from Brush in December 1964, this is probably not the first time that the two Class 47s have stood close to each other in a workshop context. *MJS*

## ▶ 16 March

Another night view proving that the use of the camera in the dark can transform even the most mundane scene, with even the slight flaring from the overhead light adding to the whole. The driver of No 144002 prepares to restart the last train of the day from Habrough station, performing the 2100 'Metro Train' connection from Cleethorpes to Barton-on-Humber. The second of the class to be introduced, in October 1986 from BREL Derby, it was and remains here a two-car set, whereas from 144014 onwards the consist was strengthened to three cars. Neither variety has, however, totally overcome the slightly rough ride inherent in the design. The sign to the left of the cab warns motorists to slow for the level crossing, glimpsed just behind the end carriage. *MJS*

## ▼ 17 March

Barnetby station has long been a place of pilgrimage for photographers, being a location with regular and frequent trains – both passenger and freight – and infrastructure of the past – semaphores and signal box. In the early 1990s the motive power was still from an earlier era, as depicted in this view of double-headed Class 37s – Nos 37275 and 37250 – heading west with empty box wagons from Immingham Docks. Introduced as D6975 on 9 April 1965, the former was named *Stainless Pioneer* at Shepcote Lane on 16 December 1988, only to have the plates removed in May 1992. A subsequent naming saw it become *Oor Wullie* in October 1993, resplendent in all-over blue with yellow miniature snowploughs, that name having been previously worn by 37402 from 1985. No 37250, new as D6950 on 10 December 1964, was renumbered 37384 in February 1998. *MJS*

**1992**

### ▲ 17 March

Equipment not frequently seen in depots – but hinting at local problems? – Frodingham's sand dispensers, looking like creatures from *The War of the Worlds* and out of use by the time of this view, frame No 20185 standing outside the shed building. Sadly, it was not just the sanders that were near the end of their useful lives, as the Class 20 was on its last legs and the depot, latterly an outpost of Immingham, was to close within a couple of years. Thankfully, although abandoned for many years thereafter, the shed building was resurrected by 2002 for use by an infrastructure company. From a design harking back to the 1955 Modernisation Plan, 20185 was new from English Electric's Vulcan Foundry on 25 February 1967, as D8185. Initially allocated to the Nottingham area, it spent many years in the Midlands, before finally finding its

way north and east. The end came, at Thornaby, on 2 October 1992. Note the proliferation of 'Stop' signs on the entrance to the shed! *MJS*

### ▼ 29 March

A wet Harrogate might have deterred many a photographer, but the huddle of intending passengers here, together with the composition of platform awning and footbridge No 45 framing the DMU and the solid northern brickwork on the left, all add up to a quiet but pleasing view of normality at this venue in the early years of the 1990s. No 141116, comprising coaches 55516 and 55536, waits at 1348 to form a service train to York. Note the similarity to their buses in this Leyland-designed unit, built at BREL Derby in October 1988. *Ray Ruffell*

**3 April**

Being in the right place at the right time – whether 'tipped off' or not – helps to capture satisfying images. Not the aesthetic quality so much this time – although the use of South Brent's signal box, the deserted sloping road and the recession to the distant hills all add to the effect – or a very rare event, but the witnessing of an eight-coach test run for spotless Nos 50033 *Glorious* and 50050 *Fearless* (alias D400) from Laira to Newton Abbot. They would both enjoy a further two years of squadron work before final withdrawal in March 1994. The location is South Brent. *Colin Marsden*

**▼ 19 April**

With the contraction of the railway and, especially, the operating locomotive fleet, long-established engine sheds suffered the ignominy of closure and demolition. Many names famous and revered among the trainspotting fraternity disappeared. While the ex-Midland shed at Leicester was not normally graced with celebrity status, it has been more fortunate than so many of its contemporaries, surviving with much of its yard space intact and even some ex-steam buildings still present into the 21st century. Over the years

loco types have come and gone, but a common feature from the late-1950s has been the visitation of examples of Brush power from nearby Loughborough. On this day, Class 60 members 60010 *Pumlumon/Plynlimon* – new in January 1991 – and 60083 *Shining Tor* – here officially just 23 days old – wait by the fuelling point between duties. The strategic placement of nameplate between post and pipe, the hose-pipe holder between post and loco, the angle of the balance weight; and the 90-degree angle from posts to rails and lines on the oil drip mat, all add to the enjoyment of the composition. *MJS*

**► 3 May**

Creeping elimination of loco-hauled trains has been a feature of our railways since the Modernisation Plan of the mid-1950s, but the process gathered pace 30 years later. Whole routes were progressively stripped of the luxury of trains comprising five, six, seven or eight coaches, to be replaced by two- or three-car DMUs with modern designs and construction methods, admittedly, but much less passenger-carrying capacity. While this might have sufficed in a climate of reducing passenger numbers, as seen in the period leading up to the era of this volume, conditions became increasingly cramped with the increase in rail travel following Privatisation. With threatening clouds adding to the occasion,

on the penultimate weekend of loco-haulage on the Oxford-Paddington route No 47441 provides ample capacity with eight coaches, as it heads the 1F20 1705 ex-Oxford service bound for London through Culham station. Having been built in February 1964, No 47441 succumbed to the inevitable, at Old Oak Common depot just five months after this view, on 15 December.

Still at Culham, ageing three-car DMU set L840, forming the 2C51 Oxford-Reading service, typifies local services over this route before displacement by 'Turbos'. The old-style footbridge and distinctive station building – here closed and not in use – make for yet another pleasing composition. *Both MJS*

Viewed from 2003, when long-distance loco-hauled trains had become a thing of the past, such sights as No 47842 (ex-*Odin*) hauling the seven-coach 1O14 1518 Manchester Piccadilly-Poole Cross-Country service past Didcot's goods yard evoke distinct nostalgia. The feeling of yesteryear is enhanced by the presence of wooden freight wagons to the right! *Odin* had an interesting career, both numerically and with identities. Starting life as D1666 on 5 March 1965, at 87E (Landore)'s

purpose-built diesel depot, it became 47081 under the TOPS regime in February 1974. Thereafter it was 47606 (22 February 1984), 47842 (22 February 1990 – six years to the day!), back to 47606 (26 March 1993), and finally (at the time of writing!) 47778. It names were *Odin* (March 1965-July 1990), *Irresistible* (July 1993) and *Duke of Edinburgh's Award* (November 2002). Just in view, beneath the tall Didcot Power Station chimney, excavations, JCBs and materials reveal work on construction of a new Didcot diesel servicing shed. *MJS*

**1992**

Also gone, under normal working conditions, is the sight on the main line of ex-Southern Region Class 33s working inter-regional freights. On this hot, sunny day, No 33063 appropriately wears Railfreight Construction decals as it drifts westwards into Reading station with an empty mineral train, watched in the shadows by an enthusiast. To the right of the gasholders, an HST set brings a train from Paddington into the station. Note how diesel spillage reflects the light on the foreground tracks. New on 6 January 1962, No 33063 was withdrawn from Stewarts Lane depot on 13 February 1997, but was sold rather than being scrapped. One subsequent home has been the East Kent Railway. *MJS*

By this date the innovation of private operators on the main line had become less of a novelty, after the initial appearance in 1986 of No 59001 *Yeoman Endeavour*, courtesy of the aggregates company. The General Motors Canada-designed locomotives still stood out from the norm, however, with their 'alien' shape and distinctive livery, their massive power but quiet operation, and their impressive reliability. Caught briefly occupying the down main line at Reading, 59001 accelerates into the station on its way back to base with a rake of Yeoman empties, between passenger trains bound for Paddington (left) and Waterloo (right). The Class 59 had received its nameplates, at Merehead, on 28 June 1986, when all four original locomotives in the fleet were so treated. Note the single white star on the front end, underneath the light cluster, identifying the loco in place of an actual number. *MJS*

**9 May**

Though a railwayman, able to access parts that others could not reach, Ray Ruffell delighted in both experiencing rail travel for its own sake and for the opportunity of a different vantage point. Thus he 'snapped' this view of Inverness depot from his carriage during a trip on 'The Orcadian'. No numbers are recorded, but an interesting variety of motive power is on hand, with No 37428 *David Lloyd George* the only one identifiable, in the centre. Note the vividly striped doors filling the arched entrances to what was in a former life Lochgorm Works.

Later on the same day 'The Orcadian' is glimpsed, lower left, at Strathcarron, during a pause while waiting for the single-track token. Ray has mounted the footbridge to capture the cause of the hold-up, No 37025 arriving over the level crossing with the 'Royal Scotsman' train. One of the earliest English Electric Type 3s, 37025 emerged from Vulcan Foundry on 31 August 1961 as D6725, initially to go to 30A (Stratford) steam shed in London. It was one of the few to retain its original identity, after its TOPS renumbering in February 1974, without name, until the very last days of BR. Just 14 days before Privatisation it was honoured with the name *Inverness TMD Quality Assured* at Inverness. Sadly, this honour was to last just five years! *Both Ray Ruffell*

## 17 May

An innovation that was hugely popular over a number of years was the 'Steam on the Met' weekends, providing the opportunity of reliving something of the glamour of steam running over the LUL four-rail electrification lines between Harrow and Amersham/Watford. One of the many locomotives to take part was No 69621, seen here with the 'Amersham Centenary' shuttle from Harrow, passing Amersham Common, on the final approaches to the end of its journey, with appropriate destination and headboards. The 'hazy' exhaust shows that the fireman is doing his job properly! The single track seen to the left is the branch line to Chesham. Note the leafy surroundings, just 25 miles from the centre of London! Built in 1924 at Stratford, by then for the LNER although as part of Hill's original 134 GER Class 'L77' locomotives, No 69621 – designated 'N7' by the LNER – was withdrawn from Stratford in October 1962. Preservation beckoned, with a base for many years at the East Anglian Railway Museum. The loco also took part in the closing ceremony at Stratford DRS on 26 March 1991.

*MJS*

**1992**

69

**◄ 18 May**

The new order: as already seen, the new generation of DMUs displaced loco-hauled trains on the Oxford-Paddington run, the type becoming known as the 'Thames Turbos'. It looks a hot day and so it was, despite the driver attired in his jacket, as one of the breed, No 165106, drifts empty into Oxford station from the holding sidings seen in the distance, to take its place in the platform and form the 1100 service to the metropolis. Obviously brand new, its gleaming condition plain to see, the set, in line with the rest of its first 14 brethren, was not formally accepted into BR's books until July, despite having already taken many hundreds of passengers back and forth to Paddington by then! *MJS*

**▼ 19 May**

The old order: meanwhile, on the 'Berks & Hants' route, the endearingly entitled 'heritage' units maintained their tenuous grip on local services to and from Great Bedwyn. Here set L409 (consisting of 51344, 59496 and 51386) is reflected in the Kennet & Avon Canal, by the locks at Little Bedwyn, conveying shoppers on the 1105 Great Bedwyn-Reading stopper. Turbos inherited the service not long after this shot was taken. Coach 51344 was cut up at MC Metals, Glasgow, in April 1999, but the other two were more fortunate, being bought by preservationists. *MJS*

## ▶ 24 May

We have already seen Nos 50033 and 50050 on page 63, put back into prime condition for their last months of service. Less than two months on, we see them again, in company with green-liveried 50007 *Sir Edward Elgar*, in the centre, polished and with white-wall tyres in the sidings adjacent to Platform 6 of Exeter (St David's) station. Cabs empty, they have worked their last rostered Class 50-hauled BR train and they wait here, superbly illuminated by the station lighting, prior to working the empty stock of a special to Laira depot in Plymouth. The headboard reads 'The Glorious End: 1987-1992' round the outside and 'West of England. 50007: 50033: D400. Thames Valley 50 Group' in the centre. The site of the old steam shed at Exeter stands to the left, while a two-car DMU stands under the Premier Distribution shed awning. *Colin Marsden*

## ▼ 15 June

Often the juxtaposition of the unconnected can lead to a surprisingly satisfying result. Trains sandwiched between lines of trees or rolling countryside are not new; and neither are views of them close by habitation, but here the sandwich is almost of two halves of different pictures, stitched together to amplify the effect of the whole. The happy curve of the house's boundary foliage is a perfect foil and balance to No 37671 *Tre Pol and Pen* as it passes Lanjeth on a Drinnick Mill-St Blazey trip working, and the placing of the two main areas of interest on the 'golden thirds' has completed the composition's success. New as D6947 on 22 October 1964, to Newport (Ebbw Junction) shed, its first renumbering was to TOPS 37247 in April 1974. This was then amended to 37671 on 9 July 1987, with the name being added at Laira a month later. The loco again became anonymous in 1999. *Colin Marsden*

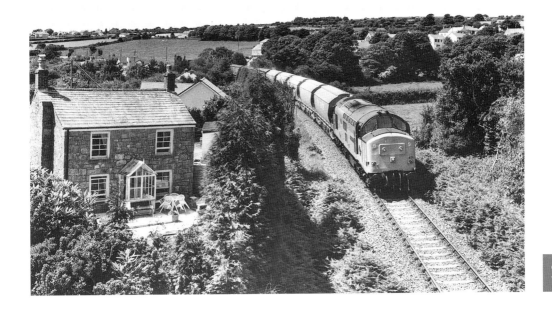

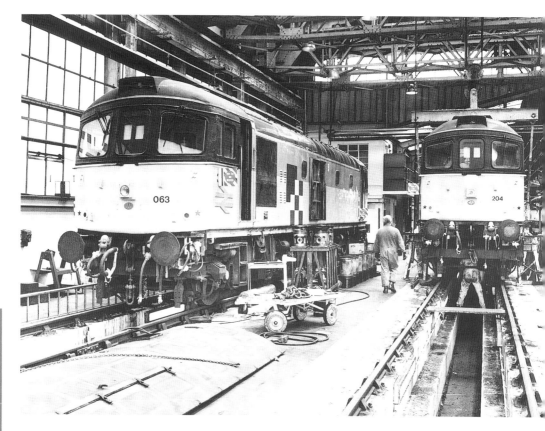

**◀ 27 June**

Although both depot locations and the engines they serviced were fewer in number after the demise of steam, visits to such installations were still fascinating and often rewarding, providing the chance to witness elements of BR with its mask down. Stewarts Lane, in southern London, was ever a place of pilgrimage for the spotter, and even on this date, with the two Class 33s receiving attention as well as the other locomotives on shed, this enthusiast was well pleased. No 33063 (left) already seen at Reading on page 66, is in for a major overhaul,

with piston-valves problem – note the cylinders on the bench – while its neighbour, February 1962-vintage 'Slim Jim' No 33204, is incapacitated with a wheel change. Initially withdrawn in October 1993, '204 was re-instated three months later, to serve another three years, before final withdrawal, from Stewarts Lane, on 13 February 1997. Note how both wear the steam-style 73A shedplate once appropriate to this London location, a practice almost unique to this depot and one that was frowned upon in certain official circles. *MJS*

**1992**

**◀ 28 June**

Down by the seaside! Mid-morning on Margate station on a Sunday was a quiet time, unlike the bedlam of holidaymakers coming and going. Here No 1535, framed by the platform awning and squat brick buildings, waits in Platform 2 to form the 1120 service to nearby Ramsgate. *MJS*

**▲ 6 July**

In this book, and railway publications generally, the freight train is in the minority. While some passenger turns can be aesthetically attractive and even glamorous, freight trains probably had more inherent variety, but there were/are fewer of them – and not having strict timetables in the same way as 'people carriers', being in the right place at the right time with a camera was much more hit and miss. Here, however, the photographer has certainly qualified, not only having the right lighting conditions and an unobstructed view, but he has also waited his moment to capture the snaking of the train to good effect. Painted in Trainload Coal livery, No 56100 passes Milford with a southbound mgr coal train from Selby Drift Mine, dust from the 36 open coal wagons mixing in the atmosphere with the locomotive's exhaust. Note the lines of wagons waiting their turn in the sidings in the left distance. *Colin Marsden*

## ▲ 15 August

One of the skills of a modern railway photographer is to make the humdrum seem somehow special and/or interesting. Potentially a 'bog-standard' loco portrait, this view of No 86208 *City of Chester* at Manchester Piccadilly has successfully used accepted composition, strong lighting, a strategically placed and obviously unposed human, and the curving and diminishing roof spans to make a strong picture. The overhead cables and gantry also serve to mask a bland sky. Pantograph at the ready, the train is the 1318 to Birmingham International. No 86208 first saw life as E3141 on 16 February 1966, being renumbered in August 1973. The name was applied at Chester on 7 March 1979. *Tom Heavyside*

## ▼ 29 August

The same photographer has again used accepted photographic elements to craft a strong image from seemingly far from ideal conditions. The light is flat and the threatening, overcast sky does nothing to lift the potential, but the use of the dark locomotive against the much lighter hillside background – captured at just the right spot on the bridge – together with the attractive pier reflections and the diagonal angle of the water leading us into the view, have all overcome the disadvantages. Even the white house on 'yonder bank' is in exactly the right place! No 37424 *Isle of Mull* crosses the bridge on the approaches to Crianlarich with the 0900 Fort William-Glasgow service. The locomotive was previously named *Glendarroch* (at Glasgow Queen Street on 9 December 1987), but for a mere ten months; the *Mull* plates were applied at Eastfield depot in March 1990, but even these only lasted just over four and a half years! *Tom Heavyside*

### ▲ 31 August

Skegness has long been a happy holiday destination, the railways using the Jolly Fisherman's 'It's so bracing' slogan since the earliest years of the 20th century. Despite the reduction in local lines, incoming trains and platform capacity, the town still receives thousands of visitors each year. Sadly, many now arrive/depart by car, but on this day two Regional Railways Summer Saturday extras wait in the station to return their loads to the Midlands and South Yorkshire, the traditional origination points for the regulars. No 47330 *Amlwch Freighter/Trên Nwyddan Amlwch* (left) will be the 1710 eight-coach train to Sheffield, while borrowed Civil Engineer's Class 31/5 No 31512 (right) double-heads 31174 on what will become the equally long

1810 to Derby. Single-car 153357 waits to the right, to be the local 1615 service to Lincoln Central. *Brian Morrison*

### ▼ 3 September

The North West of Scotland is another favourite holiday destination, but of a wholly different character. Seemingly dwarfed by both the tree on the left and the isolated 'kirk' beyond, No 37423 *Sir Murray Morrison* passes the rugged and towering surroundings at Polnish with the four-coach 1205 Fort William-Mallaig service. New as D6996 from Vulcan Foundry on 16 July 1965, 37423 was originally TOPS 37296, being renumbered into the ETH fleet on 23 January 1986. It was named at Fort William on 18 May 1988, and withdrawal was in November 1999. *Tom Heavyside*

**▲ 7 September**

Again cleverly using the available infrastructure and classic photographic elements to overcome an unflattering prospect, the photographer has here made an ordinary and potentially boring scene into one of real merit and one that again proves that, in certain circumstances, black and white can score over colour for effect and a satisfactory result. On a dull, damp day, No 47675, still bearing the *Confederation of British Industry* nameplates from when it was renumbered from 47595 a year previously, arrives at Inverness with its five-coach load as the 0916 from Aberdeen, while to the left No 158714 waits to start a journey in the opposite direction.

Originally 47268 under TOPS, it was renumbered to '595 on 11 October 1983, in readiness to receive the nameplates at Glasgow Central station on 4 November. These were removed in May 1994, prior to it being again renumbered, on 20 October of that year, to 47791, following which it was given yet another named identity, *Orient Express*, at Victoria station on 13 December 1994. Interestingly, in 1990, when new, 158714 was used to test clearances for the units between Salisbury and Exeter and in the Cardiff area, fitted with video cameras. *Tom Heavyside*

**▼ 15 September**

At the other end of the country, remnants of the past survive at Sutton Bridge Junction, as Nos 37293 and 37042 double-head a Llanwern-Shotton steel coil train northwards. Apart from the locos' liveries, the more modern wagons and the two signs, the view could almost have come from any time in the previous 30 years. The younger of the two locos, '293 was new on 1 July 1965, initially to 86A Newport (Ebbw Junction) shed, while its younger 'sibling' was from 15 June 1962, a 41A (Darnall) allocation being its first home. Neither has worn any names. *Colin Marsden*

## ▲ 3 October

Damn, I've missed it! A lone passenger stands at the end of Darlington station, looking forlornly into the drizzle and possibly wondering what to do next. Once again, the framing of the station canopy and end screen, the use of overhead electrics to mask the empty sky and the strategic positioning of the figure add up to a strong image from unpromising disparate elements. The highlights of the rails also play their part, etching in some interest into what otherwise would have been a blank bottom left-hand corner. The Victorian overall trainshed is a graphic illustration of what is lacking in protective waiting accommodation in so many of our modernised stations. *MJS*

## ▼ 3 October

It has been said before, that just because the weather is inclement or it is night-time, that is no reason to put away the camera. Wet platforms, especially, can create 'something from nothing', as they do here, light patterns on the platform's uneven surface reflecting illumination from the train and station and, in turn, throwing some light back on the constituent parts of the picture. Four-year-old 156426 waits in a dank bay platform at Carlisle before starting out on an evening service to Barrow. *MJS*

**▲ 15 October**

The clouds gather and partially obliterate the sun as the power car at the head of the 0838 Leeds-St Pancras revs up at the far end of Platform 2 to restart the journey, having paused at Wellingborough. The guard checks all is satisfactory as No 43077, in long-service InterCity livery, trails with a distinct lean on the camber. Note the survival of the ex-Midland station building adjoining Platform 1, with its attractive carved barge-boards – and there is even an ancient porter's trolley visible – while so much else of its previous history and infrastructure has been swept away here. Note also that the wooden trolley on this platform is obviously a permanent fixture, not just because of the flower arrangement, but because the handle is securely wrapped around the lamp standard! *MJS*

**◀ 31 October**

The lifeblood of passenger trains is, of course, the travelling public. This was not always fully appreciated during the BR days, when so often the railway was seemingly run for the engineer rather than the customer. Too often, passengers had to endure dirty, late and/or unreliable trains, with those journeying to and from work in the South East of England sometimes suffering worst. Here, a commuter is settled and engrossed in his copy of the *Sun* newspaper, apparently at peace waiting for his train to move from Shoeburyness and head for Fenchurch Street on the 'Misery Line', the London, Tilbury & Southend route. *MJS*

### 14 November

Many photographers – including all too often your author – look but do not see. Actually taking time and effort to really see what is in the viewfinder – especially including elements that will detract from the final image – can lead to great rewards. Here, the photographer has obviously done just that. He has captioned it 'Photograph of the year?' because of the newsworthy happenings, but the clever high positioning and repetition of the shape of the two trains leads to a very satisfying image in its own right. No 60040 *Brecon Beacons*, a distinctly unusual class of motive power for this location, leaves Waterloo, double-headed with No 33114 *Ashford 150* on the 0930 'Mule and Otter Axeman' special bound for Okehampton and Meldon Quarry, while in the foreground No 33202 *The Burma Star* carefully negotiates the first train into the new Eurostar terminal. Few other enthusiasts appear to be witnessing either event! Note the comparison between clean and open tracks into the new terminal, compared with the complex of sinuous turnouts and crossings elsewhere. *Brian Morrison*

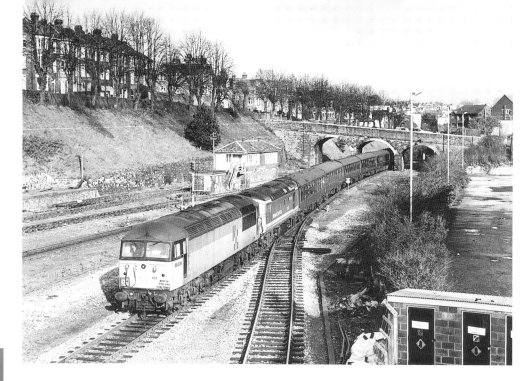

**▲ 15 November**

Having arrived in the West Country with the tour seen on the previous page, No 33114 was commandeered the following day to be back there again! This time seen arriving at Exeter Central station, the Network SouthEast-liveried Class 33 is in company with Railfreight Construction-liveried No 56039, as they head the DC Tours' 'West of England Coal Power' Waterloo-Exeter special. Bereft of its name here, the Class 56, built in 1978, was adorned with *ABP Port of Hull* in July 1994 – the first Loadhaul-liveried locomotive to be named – only to lose the distinction within three years! Despite being an enthusiasts' special, comprising at least nine coaches, there are but two heads visible from windows – a rare sight on such occasions! In the background terraced housing of varying ages spreads out across the upper part of Exeter. *Colin Marsden*

**▼ 7 December**

An interesting symphony of shapes: looking like some fat caterpillar snaking its way along the tracks, recently arrived 'Networkers' 465218 and 465216 approach Dartford as the 1049 Gravesend-Charing Cross service via Sidcup. The first of the class to enter timetabled public service were 465214 and 465215 on 13 October. As a backcloth, the Queen Elizabeth II road bridge, taking the M25 over the Thames, looks distinctly spindly and potentially hazardous from this foreshortened view. Once again, the photographer has found and used his vantage point to superb effect, enhancing the image with the long zoom, even succeeding in making the lowering sky look as though the bridge towers are supporting it. Come the rush-hour period, the bridge will most definitely not be this quiet! *Brian Morrison*

# 1993

**30 January**

Compared to the 'good old days', Liverpool Street station is now clean and airy, and as well as having platforms altered in length, it has conformed in many ways to the shifting requirements of modern society and travel. The subject of a six-year development project, it was formally opened by HM the Queen on 5 December 1991. Evidence of just one of these changes is seen starkly depicted in the sign warning that alcohol will not be allowed on certain trains on this date. No

86232 *Norwich Festival* stands in Platform 8 at one end of stock that will be affected by this ruling, as it will form the 1230 express to Norwich, one of the trains quoted on the notice. No 86232 was previously the proud owner of nameplates honouring an erstwhile Prime Minister – *Harold Macmillan* – having been thus named at Euston on 8 October 1979. Almost exactly 11 years later, on 4 October 1990, it gained the *Festival* nomenclature, and this was enhanced on 5 October 1995 to *Norfolk & Norwich Festival. MJS*

1993

81

### ▲ 4 February

Another shed and another night shot: once again, the photographer graphically displays the potential for dramatic black and white images after dark – and again it has to be said that this view would not have the same impact in colour! No 47358 (left) stands outside Buxton depot, adjacent to the ex-LNWR station, in company with three Class 37s: 37677 and 'sister' 37684 are seen enjoying the bright lights within, while 37428 *David Lloyd George* temporarily rests in the siding between the shed building and the station running line. A fitter quietly works on 37684 in the area that a few years earlier had been the sole domain of DMUs, with locomotives not allowed within the building. In July 1994 No 47358 was graced with the unofficial name of *Ivanhoe* at Tinsley depot. Since this view, the depot seen here was abandoned in favour of locomotives being stabled 'in the countryside' at Great Rocks. *Colin Marsden*

### ▼ 12 March

Whenever steam ventures out on to the main line, crowds gather to witness the vision from the past. Whether it be one of the famous and/or glamorous engines at the head of the train, or an unadvertised outing as here, the public's reception is equally fascinated in seeing these 'dinosaurs' as they slake our thirst for nostalgia. Note the young child and babes in arms, brought to wonder at this marvel! Ex-British Railways Standard 2-6-4T No 80080 – artificially wearing a 5B (Crewe South) shedplate and of a design that brought so many to model railways in the heady days of Hornby three-rail in the 1950s – stands at Carlisle, waiting to double as the 1320 all-stations to Kirkby Stephen and a driver training run. Alongside, 156448 stands in Platform 5, waiting to be a service to Middlesbrough. *Tom Heavyside*

## ▲ 15 March
Overnight stabling of 158764 provides additional evidence for two themes already examined in this book – the benefit of keeping the camera to hand after dark and the abandonment of several loco-hauled coaches in favour of a two-coach DMU for a long run. Seen in Platform 4 of Cleethorpes station, the once-titled 'Express' Cross-Country unit has the doors tightly locked and is stabled as empty stock, despite the destination and headlights, and will not move until it forms the 0712 train to Manchester Piccadilly in the morning. Comprising cars 52764 and 57764, the set emerged from BREL Derby in December 1991, one of 173 such pairings that were introduced by BR for numerous routes. *MJS*

## ▶ 16 March
Many locations that once saw much work or gave home to many examples and types of motive power and other stock have disappeared from our railway map. Places that once drew enthusiasts from far and wide and definitely seemed to be part of the 'permanent way', now have gone altogether or have dwindled to be embarrassing legacies of a proud past. Names like Stratford, Swindon and March immediately spring to mind, where it can be difficult to imagine what once was. Tinsley is another such case. As well as the massive marshalling yard now devoid of its once bustling traffic, the diesel depot has also 'gone the way of all flesh'. Built as a modern post-steam replacement for nearby Sheffield (Darnall) engine shed, on this date it was still an active powerhouse and a Mecca for number-crunchers. No 37045 slowly drifts towards the fuelling point, still bearing the nose-end twin light-boxes and doorway from its original design way back in July 1962, when it had become one of Darnall's complement. *MJS*

**17 March**

In contrast to the myriad of locations where modernisation has swept away so much of our railway past, there are pockets stubbornly clinging to the past, each a glimpse of what has gone from so many places. Apart from the modern architecture framing this shot, ageing twin-unit TO58, the semaphore signals and the glimpse of a signal box could all have come, Tardis-like, from a bygone era. While colour lights are undoubtedly superior in many ways from an operational point of view, they are soulless compared with the aesthetic delights of semaphores! With the destination blind looking distinctly the worse for wear, the empty unit slips out of Lincoln station bound for sidings to the west of the station. Shoppers patiently wait for the level crossing to re-open. *MJS*

## ▲ 17 March

Two more views of 'time-warp' Lincoln on the same day. The once-designated Lincoln (Central) station was graced in steam days with a level crossing at both ends of the station complex, frequently disrupting road traffic as the constant flow of passenger and freight trains claimed access. The east-end facility was dispensed with many years ago, replaced by a road overbridge – seen in the distance – but that at the western end still remains to impede and frustrate. High Street signal box stands guard over lifting barriers now, as opposed to the former swing gates, but still controls rail entrance and exit by semaphore signals; the attractive ex-Great Northern station building stands proudly, with its instantly recognisable tower; and, as icing on the cake, ex-BR shunter D3167 rests on an isolated length of track, as some form of tableau. The two shoppers march steadfastly on their way, each weighed down by their bags.

## ▼ 17 March

East Holmes signal box stands a mere hundred yards or so west of the station and the area is another reminder of days past. In addition to the ex-GNR box (dating from c1873!) and work-weary wooden hut, semaphores are again in evidence in the sidings on the left, which in turn give access to the ex-steam locomotive shed, once home to many steam engines and, as 40A, the proud 'master' shed for all those in the surrounding Lincolnshire countryside. No 153379, formed of coach 57329 in February 1992 and previously half of set 155329 of April 1988, passes the box as the 0908 Cleethorpes-Newark Northgate 'local', while beyond No 60002 *Capability Brown* stands on the down road, awaiting access to the station and beyond. The Class 60 was built at Brush and named there in August 1989, but not officially accepted into BR stock until 8 December 1992! *Both MJS*

1993

**19 March**

The master of the carefully chosen high vantage point and interesting shapes within the picture strikes again! Almost a trademark of this photographer – and one that has rightly marked him out as one of the top railway photographers in the country – Brian has again converted the ordinary into the visually appealing by clever use of timing, perspective, composition and lighting. How many of us would have chosen to take this picture? Seen from the 19th floor of a nearby tower block, No 207001 crosses the River Thames over Cremorne Viaduct as it forms the 1727 'Kenny Belle' Kensington Olympia-Clapham Junction service. The cessation of EMUs on these peak-hour-only trains had brought extended life to these DEMUs in this part of London, and saw '001 past its 30th birthday. Note the juxtaposition of 'ancient and modern' – gasholders and new state-of-the-art Chelsea luxury flats. *Brian Morrison*

**▲ 27 March**

'It's not really heavy, chaps, but hurry up with your pictures!' Depot boss Tony Francis pretends to be a contender for BR's strongest man, standing in the yard of Selhurst Level 5 for invited guests, four days before closure of the facility and the naming – to mark the event – of No 73003, here seen repainted into original BR green condition as E6003. Note the appropriate headcode lettering! Emerging from BR's Eastleigh Works on 27 April 1962 with the 'E' prefix denoting it to be an electric locomotive within the then numbering scheme, it became TOPS 73003 in February 1974. Originally allocated to 73A (Stewarts Lane) shed, it stayed a resident of that facility for many years, finally succumbing to changing work patterns and age on BR on 24 September 1996. Thankfully, it has avoided the 'grim reaper', to see preservation on the Lavender Line at Isfield. *MJS*

**▼ 27 March**

A slightly unusual view of Clapham Junction station and adjacent yard: away from the constant stream of trains and the public hustle and bustle, newly arrived 'Networker' 465237 (with coach 65786 visible) is espied from Platform 7 at 1326, poking out of No 7 road of the carriage shed. Note the jumble of ageing buildings beyond the far end of the shed. *MJS*

◀ **27 March**

The arrival of the 'Networkers' accelerated the withdrawal of old slam-door stock from many services in and around London. To recognise and mark the fact, the Southern Electric Group ran a 'past, present and future' tour, using appropriate coaching stock, under the banner of the 'Three Spirits Tour'. Representing the past, as announced by the boldly displayed headboard, preserved set 5001, in pristine condition, with DMBS coach S14002S leading, stands in one of the terminal platforms at London Bridge, before setting off for Victoria via a *very* circuitous route. Incredibly, this four-car 4EPB set first saw life in December 1951, then state-of-the-art! A solitary head pokes from the coaching stock. To the right is a comparison of front-end design in unit 5810 from the early 1980s. *MJS*

◀ **30 March**

Here he goes again! Once more our intrepid photographer has chosen a distinctive vantage point to depict a particular location and occasion. On the left, 1986-vintage 'Sprinter' 150138 stands in the newly opened Manchester Airport station, as one of the first passenger trains into the new facility. Its train had originated at Blackpool, whilst 1991-introduced 158809 (right) had come much further, from Scarborough. The two trains had been run as specials, as previews of airport services. Note the wings and flying buttresses echoing aspects of the Airport's raison d'être, and the high-rise Hilton Hotel in the left distance. *Brian Morrison*

▲ **3 April**

If the general public were able to witness at first hand the sheer scale and logistical nightmare that is inherent in railway infrastructure work, they would not be so quick to criticise and complain. Many, I am sure – if they think at all – imagine the network as some kind of giant model layout, where track and trains can literally be picked up and put in place! Would that it were so. Some of the logistical problems can be judged from this view of work upgrading London Transport track at Northwood Hills, between Pinner and Moor Park. Cravens-built A60 stock, on the left, passes with a Metropolitan Line train from Aldgate to Amersham, while ageing Class 20s proliferate on ballast trains. No 20007 – dating from September 1957! – with 20138 at the rear, heads towards the photographer on the centre road, removing a load of displaced ballast, while on the right No 20227 – from February 1968 – with 20110 at the rear, has ballast removed by road/railers. Note the development of front ends over the years. Sadly, despite the need for the work, there were constant complaints of noise from local residents! *Brian Morrison*

1993

89

**▼ 15 April**

Another example of an advantageous use of elevation for dramatic effect, but from a different photographer this time. No 31421 *Wigan Pier*, in Regional Railways livery, pauses at Hartford's Platform 2 while working the 1322 Crewe-Liverpool local service. A small knot of people ascends the staircase, having just detrained. Note the 1970s/80s-style design for the station buildings. Built at Brush as D5558 on

22 October 1959 and allocated initially to 32B (Ipswich) steam shed, the loco wandered around East Anglia and Lincolnshire depots until the 1970s. Under TOPS it became 31140 in March 1974, then, in fairly quick time, upgraded to 31421 on 2 November of that year, by that time being a Midland Region locomotive. Its naming came at Crewe in February 1993. *Tom Heavyside*

**▶ 24 April**

Here's another loco-hauled train, but a much longer one that that seen above. No 47528 *The Queen's Own Mercian Yeomanry* is the centre of attention, pressed into action as power for the diverted 1118 Glasgow-Euston express, as it passes the delightfully restored ex-Midland station at Settle. Twenty years the DVT's senior, '528 was named at Worcester on 10 November 1989. Comprised of stock more normally running 'under the juice' on the WCML, with the DVT immediately behind the Class 47, the diversion over the Settle & Carlisle line necessitated the provision of diesel traction. A couple stand outside offices of 'The Friends of the Settle-Carlisle Line', situated in the station building – note the advertising material positioned outside.

While many photographic pundits will opine 'Get in close',

there are occasions when this is not appropriate. Providing you 'fill the frame', long views such as the second one taken on this day can have equally dramatic results. Once more with a diverted WCML train on the Settle & Carlisle, the ruggedly awesome Ribblehead Viaduct is the setting for No 47501 *Craftsman*, in Res livery, having its 5 minutes of fame, hauling the DVT and coaching stock of the 1215 Euston-Glasgow. Named at Paddington on 22 October 1987, the Class 47 was withdrawn from stock on 12 July 2002, 36 years and two weeks after its introduction as D1944. It was subsequently bought by DRS for its locomotive fleet and, after overhaul at Alstom's Works in Glasgow, was to return to service in the late summer of 2003. Dwarfing the train above it, the magnificent structure displays the skill and artistry of the navvies that built the viaduct for the Midland Railway. *Both Tom Heavyside*

No 80080, seen previously at Carlisle, is again the object attention out on the main line. Leaving Nottingham with a motley collection of Mk II coaching stock, 'The Jolly Fisherman' headboard leaves no doubts that the train is full of Bank Holiday trippers bound for Skegness! While much of the infrastructure survives, especially the sidings and stabling point to the left, note how much has been abandoned on the right. One wonders if the boarded signal box, to the right of 80080's smoke, has since managed to avoid destruction, perhaps by sale to a preservation movement. Note also the deserted warehousing on the extreme right. *Tom Heavyside*

**1993**

### ◀ 13 May

All areas of our railway see new stock from time to time, but none can have the difficulty of introduction as that on the Waterloo & City line in London. Often known as 'The Drain', part of the reason can be seen from this view of the incomer on the right, alongside the much older stock. With no easy access, the new units had to be 'dropped down' into place from above! No 482502 awaits driver training before replacing the ageing 1940-built 487 stock, of which No 60, leading the rake on the left, is an example. The last run of the old stock, the 2027 service from Bank, ran on 28 May. One presumes that the photographer was not dropped in as well, or that he was claustrophobic! *Brian Morrison*

### ▲ 4 June

There are times when you see an image that is sheer visual delight, even when you do not personally know the location and/or people/things concerned. For your author, this photograph is one such. Celebrations of all manner of events are a constant fact of life and source of enjoyment on the railway system. Some have glamour literally everywhere; others are low-key. Perhaps the most successful, though, are those that truly take into account the background to the reason for the celebration and act accordingly. Here, preserved 306 unit No 017 is delightfully highlighted by the dappled sunlight and framed by the attractive architecture as it arrives at Emerson Park, operating timetabled trains as part of this line's centenary 'jolly'. Built in November 1949, the three-car unit has been retained for 'special duties' – to great effect here – here operating the 1240 Romford-Upminster service. *Brian Morrison*

**1993**

**6 June**
Here is another excellent example of not going in too close, but putting the train into its landscape context. Leaning into the curve at Aller Junction. No 37672 *Freight Transport Association* and 'sister' 37674 *William Cookworthy*, both adorned with Speedlink Distribution decals, head north

through the Devon countryside, south of Newton Abbot, with the 0855 Burngullow-Irvine 'Silver Bullet' china clay train. Named, respectively, on 14 September 1987 at Stratford-upon-Avon and Laira in May of that year, '672 lost its honour in 1997, whereas '674 gained a new identity at St Blazey TMD in December 1995, becoming *Saint Blaise Church 1445-1995*. *Colin Marsden*

## 18 June

A view across the interior of Crewe Electric Depot shows No 90018 – new in December 1988 – in Res livery, receiving attention and framed by two of the depot's lifting jacks. The mixture of shapes and patterns, together with light and shade and the grease on the jacks' grooves and the mobile hoist by the fitters, make for a satisfying composition.

Moments later No 90018 and the fitters are the close-up focus of attention, as they discuss some point of the work required. Nos 86239 *L S Lowry* (left), 90023 (right), with its own trio of fitters, and 90018 all wear the 'Not To Be Moved' warning notices. New on 19 June 1965 as E3169, No 86239 was named at Willesden on 4 October 1980. It was renumbered to 86507 on 16 December 1988, then back again seven months later! One of the first Class 86s to be withdrawn, it succumbed on 30 April 1996.

One of the more glamorous locomotives passed for main-line running is ex-LMS 'Pacific' No 46203 *Princess Margaret Rose*, seen on Carlisle Upperby depot being readied for work the following day over the Settle & Carlisle route. With work now concentrating on the tender, the engine itself is presumably ready, judging by the shimmering spotlessness of its coat. There cannot have been many occasions in normal British Railways service when it looked better than this! Built in 1935 at Crewe Works, it was withdrawn from 12A (Carlisle Kingmoor) shed in November 1962 and has been a long-term resident of the Midland Railway Centre at Butterley. Note the artificial wearing of a 66A (Polmadie) shedplate. *All MJS*

1993

**▲ 19 June**

The strategic use of the flower display to frame the train and hide some unwanted detritus on the opposite platform, coupled with the low angle, serves to enhance this view of No 37428 *David Lloyd George* as it waits at Perth's Platform 3 to form the 0705 train to Edinburgh. As well as night views, early mornings can often deliver a quality of light that is totally absent later in the day. Midsummer also gives the opportunity of capturing workings that would otherwise have been missed by the camera. An ex-WR locomotive, the Class 37 was named at Pwllheli on 16 May 1987, 15 months after being renumbered from 37281, but this was jettisoned in April 1998 for the loco to be fitted with *The Royal Scotsman* plates; these also did not last too long, coming off in April 2001. A new name of *Loch Long/Loch Awe* was applied in May 2002! *MJS*

**▼ 19 June**

Again, a raised vantage point – here coupled with a wide-angled lens – helps to dramatise an otherwise ordinary situation. With power car number emblazoned across its front, No 43113 *City of Newcastle upon Tyne* slows for the stop at Pitlochry, heading the 0750 Inverness-King's Cross 'The Highland Chieftain'. The driver looks very comfortable in his jumper and dark glasses, obviously at ease at the helm of his 1979-vintage power car. Initially given this name at Newcastle Central station on 26 April 1983 – the first HST power car to be named – it was removed in February 1989, re-fitted exactly four years later and removed again in April 1997! Without the suffix '*upon Tyne*', the name is now carried by GNER's No 91130. *MJS*

**▲ 19 June**

The final years of BR saw many new liveries, not just on coaching stock but also on locomotives, with some even reverting to what passed as the original livery. One such was No 26007, here 'restored' as D5300, complete with early BR bodyside stripe, seen in the yard at the side of Inverness depot. New from Birmingham Railway & Carriage Works on 30 July 1958, and allocated to 34B (Hornsey) shed, it was shipped, together with the rest of the first 20 of the class, to Scotland in 1960, going to 64B (Haymarket) on 7 May.

Becoming 26007 under TOPS in April 1974, it was eventually withdrawn from Inverness depot on 4 October 1993, less than three months after this view. Behind are Nos 37683 and 37051. *MJS*

**▼ 20 June**

A rose between thorns? Providing an interesting comparison of front ends, HST power car 43180 (of November 1981) draws its rake forward at Heaton depot, between ECML DVTs 82216 and 82229 of a decade later. *MJS*

A welcome, pin-sharp view of two ageing locomotives hard at work on a short seven-wagon ballast train. No 31270, in Railfreight Coal livery, leads 31190, in 'Dutch' grey and yellow, through the Derbyshire countryside and across the turnout at Great Rocks Junction, to work 'wrong line' on the way to a possession. Judging by the visible exhaust, it would appear that the latter locomotive is doing the lion's share of the work! No 31270 was built in June 1961 as D5800, destination 31B (Ipswich). It stayed there for many years before spreading its wings and ending up in the North West. No 31190 enjoyed a similar existence, after first seeing life as D5613 in May 1960 at 34G (Finsbury Park), before being withdrawn on 19 January 1999. Re-instated 17 months later, in June 2000, it was graced with *Gryphon* nameplates at Tyseley on the 10th of that month. At the time of writing, it was yet another of the Fragonset fleet. *Colin Marsden*

▼ **8 July**

With the influx of new units, older ex-SR EMU slam-doors saw their days end. At this date, only five Class 414/3 2HAPs survived, being used on the morning and evening Kent Coast services to supplement the standard eight-car combinations. Here No 4311 makes the scheduled Waterloo East stop, leading Nos 1808 and 1617 and forming the 1448 Margate-Charing Cross service. The 2HAP had joined the other two at Tonbridge, from where it had worked off-peak Medway Valley trains. This threesome will later form the 1713 Charing Cross-Margate commuter train. Initially set 6089 of August 1959, 4311 assumed that identity in July 1987. Note the early-evening commuters gathering for their trains home, and the rather ugly and soulless office block and high-rise flats as backdrop. *Brian Morrison*

**▲ 8 August**

When Uffington station site was remodelled in 1897, the land to the south of the then new road overbridge contained a milk dock and attendant siding. Despite the closure of the Faringdon branch and Uffington station itself in 1963, this situation pertained well towards its centenary. A rude redevelopment came, however, in 1993, with the clearing of the site to provide working access in connection with the replacement of crossovers to the north of the old station site. A partially completed turn-out panel here stands on the site of the old dock as No 37372 stands on the down main line alongside 37264 on the near-empty infrastructure train, during an engineer's possession. These occupations took place each Saturday night to Monday morning during the month of August. The two loop lines were lifted in early 1996. *MJS*

**► 15 August**

A bane of modern life, not least on the railway, is spray-can graffiti. Though not apparent here, Crystal Palace station had suffered at the hands of the 'artists' on this day, as has No 456024, albeit with a localised 'headband'! Watched by a handful of waiting passengers on Platform 1, the 1422 Victoria-West Croydon slows for the station stop, with the prominent televisual aids, to the right of the cab, ready to assist the 'Driver Only' operation. Again, the surrounding architecture does little to lift the soul! The Class 456s were introduced by Network SouthEast in 1991, providing a step-change of comfort and acceleration for South London Line commuters. *MJS*

**15 August**

The foreground weeds say it all – this is not a mainstream site! The fortunes of Strawberry Hill depot swung back and forth during the 1990s, being slated for closure on more than one occasion. Happily, it has survived, part of the depot buildings still providing a link with its L&SWR ancestry. Use at the date of this view was very much for the stabling of new stock and its testing over the nearby Shepperton branch. Seen past the weeds are (l-r) ADB977385 (electric departmental, ex-coach M61148), 930030, 932054, 466001, 465301 and 466012 – truly a mixture of old and new! *MJS*

### ▲ 16 September

Reference has been made earlier to the passing of the once mighty Tinsley depot, and evidence is here seen of the run-down in servicing work, especially, that preceded the end. In glorious isolation, No 37238 *'Spitfire II'* stands at the mouth of the southern end of the depot, the subject of some minor attention. New on 12 June 1964, as D6938, its first formal allocation was to 82A (Bristol Bath Road) on 20 July, before moving into South Wales. It gained its TOPS identity in February 1974. Once again, the placing of the locomotive within its context and the juxtaposition of light and shade lead to a satisfying image. *MJS*

### ▼ 19 September

Bletchley is one depot that rarely features in photographic collections. Possibly this was because of the usual humdrum nature of its allocation and the lack of any obvious locational highlights. However, during 1993 it was home to a collection of brand new Class 323 and 321 units, which had been suffering from teething troubles preventing them entering service. Here displaying the evolution of front-end design, 321419 stands in the yard waiting the first call, while sets L231 and L233 are sidelined at the end of the sidings. No 08484 keeps them company; a derivative of a much older design, the shunter was new from Crewe Works on 10 October 1958 as D3599. It was nearly a month before it moved to 81A (Old Oak Common), its first home. Together with 'sisters' D3600-02, similarly allocated, it stayed at Old Oak until the 1970s, when it became 08484 under TOPS. *MJS*

## ▲ 5 October

As well as new fleet liveries, there was the occasional 'one-off', where locomotives were chosen to wear new coats (of sometimes many colours). For the 'Freight**connection**' exhibition at Trafford Park Euroterminal, to mark the opening of the £11 million facility, four Class 90s were given unique branding to recognise the European railway connection. Posed for their portraits under the massive Railfreight Distribution gantry are (l-r) Nos 90022 Freight**connection**, 90130 Fret**connection**, 90128 Vracht**verbinding** and 90129 Fracht**verbindungen**. They had all received their names at Birmingham NEC the previous month, on 3 September. The last three would all receive new nomenclatures during 2000. *Brian Morrison*

## ▼ 7 October

Dawn at Charing Cross sees two 2EPB sets very close to the end of their working days. Providing anagrams of each other, 6320 (left), an ex-North London Line 'Dartmoor Unit', heads the 0644 to Gravesend via Sidcup, while 6230 will be the 0648 to Sevenoaks. Shyly hiding in the distance is 4EPB 5472, which has formed the 0603 arrival from Dartford via Sidcup. Initially 5655 in October 1959, 6320 assumed its new identity in July 1984; it was cut up at Gwent Demolition's site at Margam, in South Wales, in March 1995. No 6230 was originally 5730 of May 1955, becoming the higher numbering in December 1984. It too saw death at Gwent Demolition, this time in May 1994. The results of the multi-million pound scheme, placing a 14-storey office block above the station, can be seen behind. The work was completed in 1991, a year after the station celebrated its 125th anniversary! *Brian Morrison*

## ▶ 9 October

Open wide! Using a high-speed drill, the depot 'dentist' concentrates as he attacks No 43163's 'molar', giving a rare glimpse underneath the power car's skirt, prior to undertaking remedial repairs at St Philips Marsh. One of 197 of the most successful designs in BR's ownership of our railways, No 43163 entered service in August 1981 and, with most of the other members of the class, was still giving front-line service into the 21st century and comparing well with supposedly state-of-the-art newcomers! *MJS*

## ▼ 10 October

Here is a sad sight that has become all too common over the past two decades, as both locomotives and the traffic they handle have reached the end of the road. Redolent of the latter days of steam, lines of stored machines could at times litter sites throughout the country. Seemingly a waste of capital investment – especially when so many were summarily scrapped without being offered for sale – these 08s await their fate at Cardiff Canton depot. No 08836 (of November 1960) stands in company with 08804 (June 1960), 08822 (September 1960) and a string of other examples of the class. All withdrawn from Canton in May 1993, they saw reprieve and re-instatement on 4 March 1994, to be subsequently scattered to disparate locations. *MJS*

### ▲ 15 October

After the fate of withdrawn locos had been settled, all too often they saw the sad journey to the knacker's yard, where, 'in the heat and the dust', 'ruthless butchers' despatched the once proud machines to so much scrap metal. At the Glasgow site of MC Metals, No 20124 awaits its turn, already having had it innards ripped out, after its very short trip from store at the back of St Rollox Works! Another of the class stands to the left. No evidence of strict requirement for hard hats, goggles, ear-defenders or face-masks here! *Brian Morrison*

### ▼ 10 December

'Completing The Link' indeed! Redolent of those paper clip puzzles so beloved of Christmas cracker manufacturers, and to commemorate the Channel Tunnel handover by TML, the constructing company, representatives of the various parties pose for their collective photograph. Sir Robert Davidson (Balfour Beatty), on the right, strains at his link, while to his right, perhaps amused at his efforts, Joe Dwyer (Wimpey), Sir Alaistair Morton (Eurotunnel), Neville Simms (Tarmac), Tony Palmer (Taylor Woodrow) and Peter Costain (Costain) all smile at the camera. Behind is 9016, one of the Brush-built Euroshuttle freight locomotives. *Brian Morrison*

# 1994

## 8 January

The beginning of 1994 saw a major interruption to the Great Western main line, when the embankment over and alongside the A420, immediately to the east of Swindon, slipped quite dramatically, leaving, at one point, the up line close to being without solid foundation. Immediately 7,500 tonnes of rock were brought in by rail to stabilise matters, but a long-term solution eventually took several years – the final work and landscaping not being completed until 2003! On the down road, adjacent to the problem area, No 47366 waits with a rake of distinctly ageing ballast wagons. The loco is in grey livery with the large bodyside logo – and is still showing sign of its previous *The Institution of Civil Engineers* nameplate fitted at Liverpool Lime Street on 22 May 1986 and removed in September 1991. It gained a new persona on 19 March 1994, when it was honoured as *Capital Radio's Help A London Child* at Old Oak Common. Withdrawal came on 28 January 1999. *MJS*

### ▼ 5 February

Though still physically large, Old Oak Common depot is but a shadow of its former (steam) self, both in allocation and the breadth of its work. Though the 'factory', behind, closed on 27 March 1993, the yard still at times played host to interesting motive power – as well as the occasional Open Day. The 'factory' building here provides a backdrop to Nos 47241 and 47484 *Isambard Kingdom Brunel*, the latter proudly boasting its pseudo-Great Western livery, initially applied during the somewhat truncated GWR 150 celebrations in 1986 and here showing the refurbished version applied in August 1993. The cleaners have obviously been hard at work in this view, especially as regards the white buffers, and the loco wears the ex-steam headboard from the one-time fastest train in the country. It was stripped of its name in 1999, whereas '241 became *The Silcock Express* on 3 August 1994, then *Halewood Silver Jubilee* on 12 September 1995. *Colin Marsden*

### ▼ 7 February

These latter days of BR saw testing of the new Eurostar units, before their introduction to regular services. Snaking through the west Kent countryside, No 3101 picks up the 'juice' as it leads the long rake out of Polhill Tunnel, near Dunton Green, north of Sevenoaks, with 3102 bringing up the rear, forming the 1050 North Pole Depot-Ashford test train. *Brian Morrison*

**▲ 16 February**

In the first of two views of Class 47s, enjoying different fortunes, No 47227, seemingly devoid of traction motor, windows and a cabside, stands inside the ABB Works at Crewe. The loco came new on 9 September 1965 as D1903, another Brush Type 4 allocated to 86A (Newport Ebbw Junction) shed. Staying there until the 1970s, by which time it had become 47227, it was adorned with the unofficial name *Saladin* on 9 November 1991, during a spate of such namings at Tinsley depot. Withdrawal, from Tinsley, was on 6 May 1993, and is therefore presumably in here for component recovery before scrapping. *MJS*

**▼ 23 February**

One week later, 'sister' No 47323 enjoys a wholly different occasion. Seen inching a rake of Cargowaggons through the Rover car factory site in Swindon, with the driver cautious over the quality of the track ahead, it has just been named *Rover Group Quality Assured*. In near pristine condition, freshly painted in Railfreight Distribution livery and wearing Speedlink Distribution decals and logo plaques as well as the new nameplate, it would have taken unsuspecting lineside enthusiasts by surprise. Sadly, the fame did not last long, with the nameplates being removed in October 1996, when they were transferred to 47236. *MJS*

**▲ 10 April**

Officially BR has ceased to be nine days ago, but would anyone notice? Inevitably, with such a huge organisation, visible change was not going to be overnight, thus the 'old' InterCity 'Shuttle' branding is still displayed at St Pancras, albeit a slightly odd nomenclature for express services to Midland and South Yorkshire destinations! Old and not-so-old stand in close proximity, as the massive, elaborate and decorative ex-Midland Victorian trainshed temporarily houses HST power cars Nos 43066 – not long arrived from the north – and 43101, in very clean condition, about to be trailing car on the 1100 to Sheffield. *MJS*

**▼ 10 April**

Another past and present comparison: Nos 33020 and 33040 are cast aside and 'forgotten' at Stewarts Lane – both withdrawn for nigh on 12 months – while BR's last build of freight engines is represented by the penultimate member of the Class, 60099 *Ben More Assynt*, fresh out of Brush's works in March 1992, but not accepted officially until the 18th of the following December. New as D6537 on the last day of 1960 and D6558 on 10 June 1961 respectively, Nos 33020 and 33040 spent most of their lives working from either Hither Green or Stewarts Lane depots in London and both saw the end, from the latter location, within a month of each other in the spring of 1993. Note the non-standard driver's window on 33020! *MJS*

### ▲ 22 April

An 'old soldier' comes to the rescue! BR had teething problems that delayed the introduction of Class 323 electrics in the West Midlands, but even after they entered service on 7 February, reliability was not 100 per cent. On this day, another set had failed and had to be replaced by the old order. Doing its best to coat the overhead wires with exhaust, DMU set L713 (running as a 2+1 set), in creditably clean condition, accelerates the restart of the 1424 Redditch-Lichfield Trent Valley stopper from Barnt Green, watched by another photographer. Previously the domain of DMUs, electrification of this Birmingham Cross-City route was authorised by Cecil Parkinson, then Secretary of State for Transport, on 7 February 1990. *MJS*

### ▼ 30 April

We have seen set 5001 before, at London Bridge on page 88, but here it is in the company of another celebrity. At the time of this photograph these units were the last two from a once-extensive fleet of 4EPB 415/1 slam-door stock. To commemorate their 'celebrity' status, 5001 was repainted in its original green, and 5176 in the once-ubiquitous 'BR Corporate Blue'. In gorgeous spring sunshine, they line up for their portrait at Slade Green depot. The latter unit was subsequently moved to the Mid-Hants Railway for preservation. *Brian Morrison*

**2 May**

Railtours have been popular for the past 50 years or so, especially where locomotives facing extinction and/or well-loved types are employed. Both aspects are superbly captured at a well-photographed location on this date, as Nos 20131 *Almon B Strowger* – unusually with name affixed to the cabside – and 20118, unofficially named *Vulcan*, head past the Kennet & Avon Canal at Little Bedwyn – with no heads out of the carriage windows! – on the Hertfordshire Railtours' 'The Big E', on their way from Paddington to Exeter.

Interestingly, the canal is full on either side of the lock, but low water inside the lock itself!

Later in the day, the pair is stopped in their tracks by the camera once more, again at a well-fancied photographic vantage point, with 20118 at the helm on this occasion, providing motive power for Pathfinders' 'Torbay Excursioner'. The Paignton-York charter is passing Cockwood Harbour, with a calm Exe estuary seen to the left. This time there are heads – and arms – hanging out! Judging by the boats to their right, it is low tide! *Colin Marsden*

## 6 May

Without doubt, one of *the* events of the year was the official ceremony to recognise the opening of the Channel Tunnel. Seen at Cheriton, 'le Shuttle' Bo-Bo-Bo No 9017 arrives at Platform 10, bringing both HM the Queen and France's President Mitterand back from inauguration ceremonies on the French side – sitting in the Queen's Rolls Royce! – to take part in the UK equivalent. The band is ready to 'strike up', and the size of the crowd is testimony to how special this occasion was!

Earlier in the day, the Queen and Prince Philip were taken through the Tunnel in slightly more comfort. Approaching Polhill Tunnel, in dull weather, Nos 373004 and 373003, duly emblazoned with Union Jacks, speed south through the wet Kent countryside as the 0945 Waterloo-Coquelles Eurotunnel Terminal service. *Brian Morrison/Colin Marsden*

1994

**▲ 9 May**

With the disappearance of Speedlink after 8 July 1991 and some of the railway's past core businesses, rail freight was in some turmoil in the early 1990s, but one traffic that seemed to be bucking the trend was the transhipment of various items of stock between Rover car factories! Here No 47316, unofficially named *Wren*, carefully threads its way over the remaining stub of the ex-Highworth branch out of Swindon, as it approaches the Swindon Rover plant with a rake of empty Cargowaggons from Longbridge. Presumably the trackwork needs attention, in view of the concern obviously shown by the 'man with the red flag'! New in January 1965, this Class 47 received its unofficial name at Tinsley – where else? – on 22 December 1989. To the right is the site of Coopers Metals Ltd's scrapyard – now known as European Metals. *MJS*

**▼ 12 May**

The various items of traffic originating in the Peak Forest workings also remained healthy at the time, with the tracks in the narrow corridor passing the site being constantly active. In bright late-spring sunshine, No 37509 slowly reverses a rake of empties into the sidings – at an instructed maximum speed of 4mph. Originally D6793, new from Robert Stephenson & Hawthorns Ltd on 20 February 1963, its first allocation was to 52A (Gateshead) on 16 March. Remaining a North Eastern Region loco into the 1970s, its TOPS identity of 37093 was assumed in February 1974. In July 1985 it had the distinction of being repainted in a 'police car' livery for a TV advert! Renumbering to 37509 came on 11 June 1986. Note the results of many years of quarrying in the background. *Tom Heavyside*

**▲ 15 May**

While we probably did not give it any mind at the time, we can now appreciate, looking back nearly a decade later, the variety of locomotive types still around at the end of BR. Just an ordinary view at this date, the sight of two Class 33s, in two varieties of past liveries and temporarily stabled, with on the right an ED on a rake of loaded wooden-sided wagons certainly evokes a feeling of wistful nostalgia today. Our old friend No 33063 – seen before at Reading and Stewarts Lane – in Railfreight Construction garb stands on the left, with Nos 33048 (new in August 1961) and 73105 *Quadrant* (December 1965) in Tonbridge yard. Both the 33s were withdrawn from normal active service on the same day – 13 February 1997. Beyond, a double-EMU train swings off the Sevenoaks branch and heads for the station. *MJS*

**▼ 15 May**

If for nothing else, this photograph reminds your author that this Sunday was *very* hot, and touring round southern England taking photographs was a sweaty affair! Showing that with care and forethought and the use of light and infrastructure, even the most mundane of stock can present an attractive portrait, No 5829 stands temporarily idle at 1424 in a deserted Platform 2 at Caterham station. Note the twin-sized painted 'Mind The Step' instructions! *MJS*

1994

**28 May**

Despite some closures and threats of more, there were a few straws of hope for improvement in the wind. The so-called 'Ivanhoe Line' was initially a grandiose scheme to link Derby and Burton-on-Trent by local services via Leicester. Sadly, finance and local politics precluded the worthy and valid idea, but not before the Leicester-Loughborough section had been inaugurated by Roger Freeman, Transport Minister, on the day before this view. Standing in the brand new Platform 3 at Loughborough, utilising the old down freight line, No 156422 waits to form the 1515 service to Leicester as part of the 'Ivanhoe Line Fun Day'! Note the famous name and factory to the right – as a schoolboy in the late 1950s, standing on this station waiting for my train home, I would delight in seeing new locomotives emerge from the factory on a branch that then ran into the works complex immediately to the right of the 156. A tower from the old 'Falcon' factory can be seen immediately above the unit's roof – it is not wearing a tiara!

Later on the same day, another 'Sprinter' unit, 156407, calls at Barrow-upon-Soar station as the 1600 Loughborough-Leicester duty. In previous times, Barrow had been graced with a twin-platform station a quarter of a mile or so to the north, but powers decreed that the site gave insufficient clearance for passing HSTs. Thus this new site was constructed by a narrow road on the southern edge of the village. Sadly, this mitigated against disabled access, whereas the original bore a gently sloping road from the main village street! Also, note the lack of a proper waiting shelter. *Both MJS*

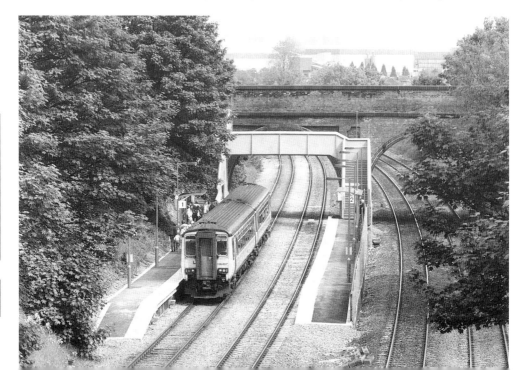

**▲ 29 May**

March has seen many changes in its railway's fortunes over the past century. Once home to the giant Whitemoor marshalling yard, a vibrant engine shed and the hub of a myriad lines radiating to all points of the compass, the place is now, as they say, 'a shadow of its former self'. Not surprisingly, all this, coupled with the station not being in the centre of habitation, has seen a reduction in patronage. On this Bank Holiday just one passenger stands ready to make use of the comforts of No 158788 at 1410, as it slows for the stop at Platform 1 on its 1250 Norwich-Liverpool Lime Street cross-country journey. Thankfully, much of the original architecture survives, giving, in conjunction with the extant semaphore signals, some vestige of permanence. *MJS*

**▼ 30 May**

Here is another new station, reviving services to a place once stripped of them. Yet again, the trains are DMU units, but rather these than nothing. The angle graphically demonstrates the staggered nature of the new build – which saw its first regular service on this day, following officially re-opening on 19th – as No 150142 arrives at Clitheroe, on the first day of the service. Note that there are proper shelters provided here and what appears to be part of the old station building – duly tarted up – is happily still present. *Tom Heavyside*

### ▲ 1 June

Old and new buildings provide the backdrop for another new service. No 158846 stands in Leicester station, on the recently revitalised Platform 1, forming the 0942 Birmingham New Street-Cambridge cross-country diagram. Against the odds, the old wooden covered passageway from the building on the right to the station, and the old mail/parcels platform and sidings, survive, despite the wholesale redevelopment of Leicester station and surrounding area – note the recently constructed 'angular toadstools' in the background! – over the previous decade. The substantial gateposts underneath the passageway are the sole remaining artefacts of the original Campbell Street terminus station, opened in 1840 and replaced by the London Road facility (seen on the left) in 1892. *MJS*

### ▼ 4 June

There are many 'behind the scenes' areas on our railway that neither the travelling public nor the average enthusiast can see under normal conditions. One such is the wheelhouse. Strategically placed in locations throughout the country, it provides a vital facility for the operations departments, able to handle both swift remedial work and more serious problems. Here No 142091, new from BREL Derby in April 1987, enters the building at Leeds (Neville Hill) depot for a spot of wheel balancing. The machinery seen in the foreground is state-of-the-art, manufactured in Switzerland. *MJS*

## ▲ 5 June

As well as the abandonment of March's marshalling yard – mentioned on page 115 – Tinsley's has seen a drastic reversal in fortunes in its facility. Once a proud hump yard – opened on 29 October 1965 by, somewhat ironically, Lord Beeching! – encompassing 145 acres and with a capacity to handle 4,000 wagons per day, it employed specifically manufactured Class 13 shunters to operate it. Changes in traffic and political views, however, reversed decisions and fortunes, denuding the tracks. The last major yard to be constructed, the hump ceased operation in December 1994, after a mere 19 years. The old control tower was once an island within a sea of rail – how times have changed! No 08813 here looks lost and forlorn standing by the side of the tower, as do the sparse strings of wagons on the right-hand, northern side of the yard. *MJS*

## ▼ 14 June

There are locations that regularly feature in published works and others that are seemingly never visited! This could be for a variety of reasons, but one is certainly isolation, away from regular through routes. Tenby is one such, on the long branch from Whitland to Pembroke. Holidaymakers and shoppers, however, are annually and regularly grateful for its presence, as seen in this view of single-car No 153380 pausing as the 0905 Swansea-Pembroke Dock service. Another creation from the splitting of a 155 unit, this example is coach 57330 from twin-car set 155330. Note the twin-language station nameboard. *Tom Heavyside*

## ▲ 27 June

As well as passenger services, freight traffic was to become an important component of Channel Tunnel business, albeit thwarted by negative non-railway influences early into the 21st century. Those days were a long way off, however, as the first ever loads were due to depart behind Nos 47053 *Dollands Moor International* and 47375 *Tinsley Traction Depot – Quality Approved*, seen at Willesden Euroterminal, duly buffed up in sparkling condition in the new Railfreight the new Railfreight Distribution livery and bearing celebratory headboards and Tinsley 'white rose' depot plaques. While this had been '375's only name, its companion had previously been *'Impala'* (unofficially applied at Tinsley on 11 July 1990) and *Cory Brothers 1842-1992* (affixed at Felixstowe on 28 September 1992). No 47053 was withdrawn from Bescot depot on 17 February 1999, but re-instated three years later, on 18 March 2002, to join the ranks of Fragonset's locomotives. *Brian Morrison*

## ▶ 7 July

Before squadron services transporting passengers between the UK and the Continent could begin, much testing had to be done. All manner of aspects of the operation were tried and inspected, with perhaps the most visual being the trial running of Eurostar units over the anticipated routes. Leaving Willesbrough Crossing, east of Ashford, No 373007 undertakes a test run to Paris Nord station. The sleek, modern, semi-bullet-like front design of the unit looks rather incongruous positioned next to the diminutive crossing control box, 'Bert's Place', with its 'Heath Robinson' salt container. The image of a high-speed train and a level crossing somehow do not fit easily together, and, indeed, the scene was transformed subsequently by the construction of an underpass! *Colin Marsden*

## 10 July

As every spotter knows, there are those locomotives that, for him or her, are rare, that seemingly manage to disappear whenever a visit is organised or a spot of lineside observation is indulged in. No 47369 was one such 'Scarlet Pimpernel' for this photographer, so when he learned during a visit to Doncaster Carr depot that it was 'hiding' within the nearby Electrification Depot, the answer was obvious. Access to the latter site proved not straightforward, however, but was eventually permitted, giving rise to this rare shot, as both the site and the train on which the locomotive is coupled were not normally captured on film. Amidst all manner of appropriate bric-a-brac, an electrification train has been marshalled, ready for use in the Bradford area electrification. New from Brush as D1888 on 30 July 1965 and first allocated to 41A (Tinsley) on 7 August, TOPS saw it change to 47369 in February 1974. Anonymous thereafter, never being named or renumbered, it was withdrawn from Immingham on 21 January 2000.

Later in the day, the embankment above the southern fringe of Knottingley depot was used to advantage to capture this collection of main-line and shunting locomotives. No 09014 stands in the foreground with a short rake of oil tanks, while elsewhere (l-r) are Nos 60088 *Buachaille Etive More*, 08605 and 08782, together with a clutch of Class 56s, including 56043, 56031 *Merehead*, 56107 and 56078. Originally D4102 of October 1961, 09014 was the preserve of the Southern Region, as were all 26 original 09s, right through to the late 1980s, when traffic demands changed there. Those coming north were initially for local trip workings, where their higher top speed was an advantage over the previously used 08s. *Both MJS*

**▲ 21 August**

In this comparison of generations of DMUs, part of the new order – and previously seen on page 18 at Loughborough – is York-built No 150150, standing in Platform 11 of Crewe station, at precisely 1318 and 5 seconds, during a quiet spell before embarking on a run along the North Wales coast as the 1420 service to Llandudno. As previously mentioned, it was the last of the class of 50 twin-car Class 150/1 units, comprising a DMSL and DMS combination and emerging from York in March 1986. *MJS*

**▼ 27 August**

Along the North Wales coast and down the Conwy Valley line from Llandudno Junction station, the (some would say unusual) bright sunshine at Blaenau Ffestiniog shows to advantage the re-liverying of No 101685 into its original green livery, with the small yellow front end the only concession to modern-day practice. Supposedly close to the end of its days, the unit was chosen to receive this atavistic cloak as a recognition and celebration of its 'heritage' status. Note that its set number is displayed on a board in the driver's window, rather than emblazoned on the front end. On the site of the Festiniog Railway's original line to Duffws, in the centre of Blaenau, this new station, with a similarly newly built FR facility off the picture to the right, was opened in 1982. *MJS*

## 30 August

The railway is not unaccustomed, nor immune, to rethinking of strategy and/or changing of plans/ideas. We have already seen the reduction in or destruction of once-proud marshalling yards, but one decision coming to fruition in these early days of the Privatised railway was that to re-open Tyne Yard. Planned to re-open as a depot, with the wagon repair works at Gateshead moved to the 'new' facility, the yard was once again on the verge of becoming a hive of industry. In this superbly composed portrait, tightly but appositely cropped, with the background pylon included to give the picture height, there is a healthy presence of both trainload and locomotive. No 37697 (ex-37243) waits to leave with its load of ballast, while Nos 56107 and 60046 *William Wilberforce* head the two roads of engines. *Brian Morrison*

### ▲ 10 September

As part of the Privatisation process, the railway freight business was split into three companies – officially from 16 October – each operating within loosely defined North East, South East and West areas of the UK. Each developed its own livery, with Transrail opting for retention of the existing double grey but with the addition of a large bodyside 'T'. This motif can clearly be seen on these two immaculately turned-out locomotives, as Nos 56044 *Cardiff Canton Quality Assured* and 60097 *Pillar* lean into the curve, heading the 1035 St Blazey-Newport ADJ past the seafront at Dawlish Warren, with the town of Dawlish in the background. Note the different opinions as to where to place the 'Transrail' legend. This was the first visit of locomotives in this livery to the West. *Colin Marsden*

### ▼ 22 September

New liveries and new stock came to the Isle of Wight during our period, the latter element in the guise of ex-1938 London Underground stock. Sets Nos 003 and 004 of Class 438 shelter from the warm sunshine inside the Ryde Works building, as an unidentified 'sister' unit waits its call to duty. Obviously the recipient of some recent rebuilding, the yard in front of tracks 1 and 2 is incredibly clean and tidy, a far cry from the state of affairs here in steam days, when all manner of railway debris could be littered around the yard. *Tom Heavyside*

### ▲ 1 October

Chaos reigns! It appears to be a quiet period at Brighton, with little happening and few impending travellers, but all is not what it seems. Temporarily 'down' due to a computer fault, all platform departure screens are blank, leaving both passengers and staff in something of a quandary as to what is to leave next and to where! At 1012 on this Sunday morning No 1863, in Platform 2, is a totally unidentified service, although doors are open and a small knot of people gather to consider their options at the far end. Meanwhile, to the left, No 1717 is supposed to be in the throes of becoming the 0930 West Worthing-Eastbourne train – but no one seemed absolutely certain at the time! *MJS*

### ▼ 1 October

Dover West Docks station had a glamorous past, handling passengers from incoming liners on their way to a myriad of destinations throughout the country. By this date, however, despite appearances, with two EMU units standing in the platforms, the station is closed and only used to berth stock between duties from Dover Priory station. The closure, effective from 24 September, meant that passengers had to travel to and from Dover Priory, with a bus connection to Eastern Docks! No 1533 stands to the left, with 3521 in the centre. Just visible above the large arched trainshed window, the legend 'SE&CR' betrays the station's origins and harks back to more halcyon days. Sadly, the superb diamond crossings in the foreground will no longer bear the weight of boat trains. *MJS*

### ▲ 2 October

Over the years, often due to the local topography, many of the early railway companies built imaginative designs. Whether it be stations, bridges and viaducts, or, as here, the 'humble' signal box, their simple presence could be a visual delight. This magnificent ex-SE&CR 1900-vintage structure at Canterbury East, raised from a restricted site to avoid passing stock, provides a superb frame to No 3192 entering the station on duty 37, the 0946 Dover Priory-Victoria, running 7 minutes late. The semaphore indicates the imminent arrival of a train bound for Dover via the Lydden Tunnel. Note the signalman's bicycle stuffed unceremoniously underneath the box steps! *MJS*

### ▼ 2 October

In conjunction with the 'Chunnel' works, Ashford station underwent massive upheaval and redesign to incorporate the Eurostar services to and from the Continent. Part of those ongoing works can be seen here in the background as No 47245 *The Institute of Export* in Railfreight Distribution livery stands in a through road on a rake of container boxes, awaiting the arrival of No 47365 *Diamond Jubilee* on an ex-Dollands Moor Freightliner test train. Contact is attempted by 'walkie-talkie', on the right. New in December 1965, '245 was the recipient of yet another unofficial name from Tinsley depot, on 19 December 1989, before receiving the title as seen here at Mossend on 8 July 1994. It was withdrawn on 19 January 1999, but re-instated from 11 February 2003. Also built in 1965, on 6 July, 47365 has led a seemingly less eventful life, gaining its name at ICI Winnington on 20 September 1986 and still 'on the books' at the time of writing. *MJS*

## ▲ 2 October

I have often said that an elevated vantage point aids railway photography. Certainly it has helped both composition and visual satisfaction in this view of No 1580, coupled to 1871, passing Gillingham signal box on an unidentified Strood-Gatwick Airport service. Although the barriers are down, the unit approaches the crossing gingerly, watched by engineer and signalman inside and outside the box, as the area is under an engineer's possession, with only hand radio signalling available. *MJS*

## ▼ 15 October

The serious head-on collision at Cowden on this day, between green-liveried 205029 and Network South Central 205018, claimed five lives and was much featured in the media, with many calls querying why two opposing trains were allowed on to the same stretch of single track, albeit in foggy conditions. In the aftermath, pieces of 205018 stand and lie forlornly, waiting collection. Coach 60817, from set 018, new from BR Eastleigh Works in October 1957, was cut up on site later in the month. No 60667 (ex-205018) and 60147 (ex-205029) were also scrapped, but the remaining three coaches of the two sets were later united into a re-vamped 205018 set. *Brian Morrison*

**1994**

### ◀ 18 October

Following the eventual success of the Brush-built Class 66s, the Loughborough Falcon Works were given the contract to build the 'look-alike' 92s for Channel Tunnel freight services. Named after famous personalities from both sides of the water, the locomotives bore the three-ringed Eurotunnel logo, as seen here at a line-up to celebrate the delivery of the type to Crewe International Electric Depot. No 92016 *Brahms* stands in the bright autumn sunshine with, next off the delivery line, 92017 *Shakespeare*. Both had their names affixed within Brush's factory the previous month, before leaving the site.

Meanwhile, later in the day and back in the factory, construction of the fleet continues apace, and already Nos 92031 and 92032 are well on their way to completion. The first of the class on to BR metals was 92002 *H G Wells* on 10 December 1993. Three members of Brush staff meet to consider a point of query on the build inside the workshops, with racks of equipment and bits of parts scattered around, awaiting their call. Nos '31 and '32 eventually entered stock on 23 June 1995, respectively named *Schiller* and *César Franck*. Both MJS, *lower courtesy of Brush Traction Ltd*

**1994**

### ▲ 15 November

Compared to the freight division of rail Privatisation, the slicing of the passenger cake was a nightmare! Compared to four freight companies, including Freightliner, 25 organisations to own and run the passenger services was a recipe for disaster. It was also a recipe for colossal expense, as all sought to establish a branding, often necessitating more than one case of re-liverying. Compared to some, however, the South Wales and West franchise was low key as regards the latter aspect, as can be seen in this view of stock inside the running shed of that company's area of Cardiff Canton depot. No 158870 (left) warms up ready to move out to Cardiff station and begin a journey to Liverpool, while 150276 and the other stock are temporarily out of service. *MJS*

# Index